IMPROVE YOUR SOCIAL SKILLS

Thirteen Keys to Success through Mastering your Emotions, Improving Conversation, Effective Communication Skills, Increasing your Empathy, and Building Self-Esteem

Dale King

© Copyright 2020 by Dale King - All rights reserved.

The following Book is reproduced below with the goal of providing information that is as accurate and reliable as possible. Regardless, purchasing this Book can be seen as consent to the fact that both the publisher and the author of this book are in no way experts on the topics discussed within and that any recommendations or suggestions that are made herein are for entertainment purposes only. Professionals should be consulted as needed prior to undertaking any of the action endorsed herein.

This declaration is deemed fair and valid by both the American Bar Association and the Committee of Publishers Association and is legally binding throughout the United States.

Furthermore, the transmission, duplication, or reproduction of any of the following work including specific information will be considered an illegal act irrespective of it is done electronically or in print. This extends to creating a secondary or tertiary copy of the work or a recorded copy and is only allowed with the express written consent from the Publisher. All additional right reserved.

The information in the following pages is broadly considered a truthful and accurate account of facts and as such, any inattention, use, or misuse of the information in question by the reader will render any resulting actions solely under their purview. There are no scenarios in which the publisher or the original author of this work can be in any fashion deemed liable for any hardship or damages that may befall them after undertaking information described herein.

Additionally, the information in the following pages is intended only for informational purposes and should thus be thought of as universal. As befitting its nature, it is presented without assurance regarding its prolonged validity or interim quality. Trademarks that are mentioned are done without written consent and can in no way be considered an endorsement from the trademark holder.

Table Of Contents

Introduction 1

Chapter 1: Choice of Words 3

    Principles of Choice of Words 6

    Ways of Improving the Words Choices 10

    Importance of Words Choice 17

Chapter 2: Anxiety: The Worry about Other People's Thoughts about Us 21

Chapter 3: The Magical Power of Words 26

    Reflection of Words Before We Speak Is Based On the Two Techniques Below; 37

    Benefits of Watching the Degree of Intensity of the Words 38

Chapter 4: Power of Words in Strengthening, Encouraging and Boosting Confidence 42

    Life Is Worthwhile If We Learn From Our Own Experience. 45

    How Your Words Can Affect Your Life 49

    You Should Offer Compliments to Others 57

Chapter 5: Words Shape the Beliefs, Values, and Destiny of a Person 60

The Causes of Difference in languages 66

Language and Culture 71

Chapter 6: Conversation: Developing Empathy by Improving Conversational Skills 78

Chapter 7: Be Interesting: Develop the Skills Of Great Successful People 86

Chapter 8: The Power of Metaphor 94

Popular Metaphors and Their Usage 97

Chapter 9: Learn To Manage Your Inner Dialogue 113

How Your Inner Dialogue Can Lead To Overall Happiness 114

Chapter 10: Love Relationship 130

Chapter 11: Develop Humor and Make New Friends 136

Chapter 12: Knowing How to Tell Stories 142

Tactics to Use to Capture Attention and Communicate Effectively 142

Chapter 13: Mindset 147

How to Use Positive Words in Your Day To Day Life 154

Conclusion 163

Introduction

The dominant means of communication is through speech. Speech is language and someone needs to be good at language because it defines how we make ourselves either understood or misunderstood by others. Sometimes, language can even make us appear ambiguous and irrelevant. This is because speaking is done under different circumstances and hence the language that one uses needs to be in conformity with the mood, occasion and mind the objective of the moment.

Yet many people get it wrong with words. Parents use the words on their children and some do not end up socializing them well. Words have ruined very promising relationships and sometimes broken families. The words that are used in communication are the reason for some of the greatest regrets that any person can talk about. It is therefore not a trivial course to delve into the matter of words and how they can influence interactions and even people.

This book dissects the whole matter of words and their influence. It acts as a guide and manual that will direct and caution. The books talk about the various ways that words have power in the lives of people. It also shows that words can be a destiny changer having just said that some promising relations have been broken because of words. This book will also discuss the way that words can determine the degree of happiness in your life. This is in the interest of demonstrating the essence of becoming more sensitive in how language is used in various communication occasions and events.

Chapter 1: Choice of Words

'Words have the power to destroy and to create. A word can change an event and a feeling. It is so important to choose the right words

Words are a way of communication. The choice of the words we use is a style of how we express ourselves be it in written words, spoken words or even what we just think in our minds. The words we use might seem insignificant, but they can create beauty in the hearts and minds of many and at the same time, they can cause irreparable havoc that forever remains in the minds of people and to go down in the books of history. Word Every person chooses the words which he feels comfortable with, which he feels are simple enough for the audience to understand and the choice of these words accurately, can make a difference between building greatness and hope or destroying by causing catastrophes.

Miscommunication of words causes big uncontainable catastrophes. Words should be well communicated to make or drive home the meaning that is intended. For everything to be successful in the world the words should be communicated clearly and the choice of the words should be wise. Successful relationships start and go further because of choice words.

Those in these relationships know when the red button has been pressed and then make sure to choose the right words to change the button to green.

Sometimes words may have very simple and little meaning attached to them but the audience misunderstands them and they end up causing great pain and even wars. The audience feels disrespected because of the misunderstanding of the words. Just like the wrong or the unsaid words can bring down a space ship, so are the misunderstood words. It is important that as much as your choice of words is good, you should be very clear and thorough. You should reflect on how the message will be conveyed and received.

The words that are unsaid hold the same importance as that of the spoken words. The silence that falls between the unsaid words and the spoken words hold a lot of significance in the message. The silence is the most powerful of all of them. The silence between the words can help sink the message in the minds and hearts of the audience. For example, a person who talks nonstop is more likely to be misunderstood, misquoted and so many other things than a person who speaks a few words which he has chosen carefully. The words we use are definite; they do not have any dynamic range or malleability unlike the interpretation of our lives. We can define our lives in whichever way because we have powers within us to change the way we live. Unfortunately, we cannot change the words we have already spoken out after some time. Especially if we said them clearly and explained them to sink in the audience's mind. Words do not have these dynamics and malleability. When dealing with words, a dog is a dog and it cannot and be a cat. If you tell someone he is stupid, you mean he is stupid, it cannot change be stupid meant good or clever.

In your choice of words, you should not go deep looking into the meaning of words. Sometimes the words are only simple and do not mean otherwise. Always look out for the added benefits of the tone, look at the facial expression and the body language of the speaker. The power of the choice words is two-way traffic. There is power in their utterance and the power in how they are ingested, so each time we speak, we write or when we think, we should be very mindful of what we are engaging ourselves into.

There is a problem when we do not take any active role in choosing the words we express. When we speak without taking into account the force created from the flow of our speeches when we allow other people's words to emotionally paralyze us and then we answer back without choosing our words carefully. Most of us, in one way or the other, are victims of the power of choice of words.

There are principles of choice of words that everyone should uphold while choosing the words to address an audience. These principles govern the choice of words so that one is able to know if his choice of words is within the complying rules or not, if not, you are always free to change your choice of words before you air them out to cause harm or complications that is irreparable.

Principles of Choice of Words

Obsolete words

Obsolete words are outdated words. Others call them archaic words though the difference between the archaic words and the obsolete word is that the obsolete word has fallen into the dilution more re4cently than the archaic word. Obsolete words are words that have been overused and now hold less meaning or impact when they are used again. They are diluted and can easily be misinterpreted. Avoid using obsolete words while speaking or writing. Your choice of words while addressing people no matter how good they are. If you use obsolete words, they will dilute the meaning of the whole speech. People will start misquoting you and they will end up misunderstanding you which later o0n will cause problems.

Emphasize positive words

As a speaker or a writer if you want your points to be understood, maintain positivity. Make sure you emphasize the positive effects of whatever the message you are addressing. You cannot start speaking about the negativity of a project when you really want that project to be implemented, you will have to talk about the positivity of that project. Also, when a speaker is talking about a certain product, he does not have to talk about the competitor of the product in a negative way, this drives a wrong message across. Could be you are jealousy. But if you maintain the positivity in your emphasis, you may just get what you need. Choice of words playing it your way and you get what you want, play it the competitors' way and you create chaos.

Avoid Overused Words

There are words that have been used more than they should actually be used. They have been overly used though they have their meaning. These words make your message so boring and they make the audience have a different judgment from you. It is either you did not prepare well or you are not conversant with the trend of the world and civilization. You cannot expect people to listen to you and agree with you when your choice of words is not to their expected standards. Some audiences expect words to reflect intelligence and if this cannot be achieved when you open your mouth giving a speech to them, they switch off completely. Make sure the choice of your words is not so repetitive in that they are everywhere.

Choose strong words

Strong words do not mean ambiguous words. It only means that you choose the words that best suit the occasion and leaves no room for alteration. Choose the words that the audience might not be expecting to hear but when they hear them, they will go along with them. Choose the words that will put smiles on their faces and alleviate tension if any. For example, you cannot go to a place where there are community wars, and start addressing people by pointing fingers at one side of the group expecting the war to end. You can point fingers yes, but at both of them. Your words should be strong enough to drive the point at home by sinking clearly without misquote or misinterpretation in the minds of the audience.

Use specific precise words

Your choice of words will depend on the audience you are addressing. You should make sure your words are directed to what you intended to communicate. They should address the point only meant to be addressed, in other words, they should be specific. For example, you have a problem in your relationship because your partner is drinking alcohol too much to extend of forfeiting the responsibilities he is expected to execute. To address this issue be exact. You want to address your partners' drunkenness, choose the words that concern drunkenness. Then be specific. The specific thing here is alcohol. Address alcohol and the effects it is causing in his life and to the relationship. You should not just start jumping from one thing to another, like the last time he bought you a dress, the last he ever took you on a date, the girl you caught him with, his annoying sectary and so many others. Maintain your choice of words by being specific and exact or precise and things will be well solved.

Understandable words

Your choice of words, whether written or spoken should be understandable. You should make sure that the audience will understand what you are saying. If you choose words in a way that you alone can understand or with a mindset that you do not care about who understands them and how they understand them, then disaster is knocking on the door. How the audience understands what you are saying or you are writing is very important. This helps in clearances of any doubt and limits any chances of misinterpretation of the message you are putting across. This also helps or gives room to quickly remedy a disaster if any arises due to your wrong cho9ice of words.

While we have principles that govern our word choices, there are ways that also help us improve our words choice and stay as relevant as possible.

Ways of Improving the Words Choices

Improve your vocabulary

You must be able to have a variety of vocabulary to use while addressing the audience. You do not want to be one-eyed when you have two. Go to libraries, read a lot, do online research and you will find that your vocabularies have increased. You will find yourself using words that you have never used before to address the audience. More vocabulary gives you ease with the message and they paint the relevancy picture in you. They make you stand out before the audience.

Use new words in a sentence for practice

If you want to improve in your choice of words, start practicing the new words. Use them in sentences when talking to friends or families. You have to familiarize yourself with words before you go out using them to new audiences and the only to do that is to practice them in the sentence then within no time you will know how they are used.

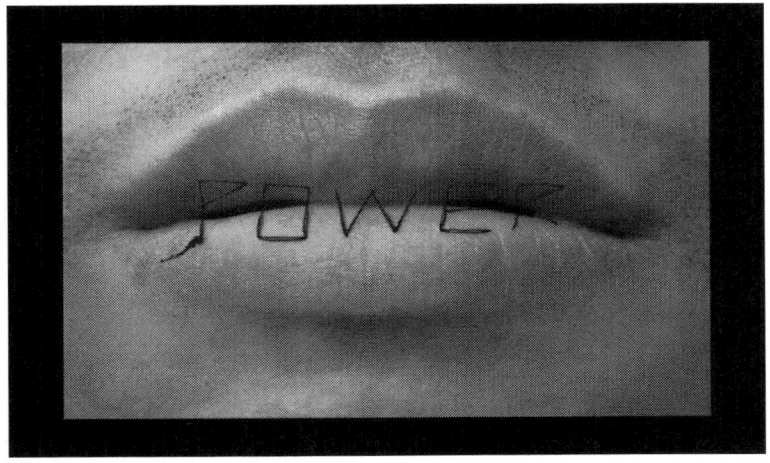

Image: Words affect

Always replace general words with specific words

You cannot generalize everything when choosing your words. This will end up sending a wrong message. Be specific. Generalization while choosing words can seem as disrespect to some people and when some people in the audience feel that they are disrespected; your message will not be conveyed. For example, if you are chosen to go to a global warming summit that is being attended by presidents, governors, senators and other junior delegates to address people in that meeting, do not generalize. Do not go about and say '"good evening ladies and gentlemen". As much as ladies and gentlemen are good but it is not good enough. Some people in that forum want their presence to be recognized. They want their titles to be recognized without generalizing them with their juniors. You can start out by the point the specifics, 'the chairman of the global warming summit of this year, the presidents of different states in the house, the governors present, the senators around and other delegates present, good evening". This will sound better to every ear that is listening to you. They will be addressed. They will feel the attachment and inclusion of what you will be telling them. So, to improve your choice of words, never generalize.

Avoid slang

Slangs are words that people consider casual ort informal. Writing slang or giving a speech in slang to different audiences is very unprofessional. Slang is mostly used in the streets. The use of slang can cause misinterpretation to the audience because slang might be localized ion one part of the society and the others do not understand its meaning. Sometimes slangs have multiple meanings and can cause confusion in the minds of people. For example, the use of the word "fuck", people use these words differently. It is slang. Some use it to mean surprise, some to mean hurt; some use it to mean the intimacy between a man and a woman. Use in the sentences:

Fuck, you came, am so excited that you remembered to visit me.—this person is surprised and happy that he was visited, he is using "fuck" to show his surprise

Fuck am going to disfigure his face—this person is hurting while using the word fuck, he is even swearing of going to hurt the other person too.

It was a good fuck darling—this could be communication between lovers or people in a relationship where one is appreciating or complimenting the other for intimacy.

Therefore, if you want to improve your choice of words and maintain relevance, you should avoid slang. People will not know what you mean and this might end up bringing problems.

Pick words that match the tone

Your choice of words and the tone matters a lot. You cannot be angry while your words are so soft. Your tone should reflect anger for someone to understand. You cannot be addressing people about the importance of growing trees while your tone is so high, people will feel that you are a dictator. You are trying to command then around and, in the end, this will fail. So how you choose your words, should be keen on the tone accompanied by it. For example, if your sibling, friend or your child tells you in a low tone, 'am sorry am not going" after sending him somewhere. You will be concerned and want to find out why he is saying that. In the same scenario, you decide to send him then and then he shouts back, " am not going". There will be mixed reactions. You will have an argument; because you will feel disrespected and even at times disciplinary measures will be taken,the tone can be either positive or negative. In this case, the first tone reflects positivity but needs concern, while the second signifies negativity that requires disciplinary intervention. Therefore, your choice of words and the tone matters a lot.

Use a dictionary to find antonyms or synonyms

If you are writing or maybe practicing on your speech, make sure, you do not repeat the same words all the time. Your speech or article will be so boring. It is advisable for you to look up synonyms of the words. You can use words with the same meaning but they are different words. In a case where you take your trouser to the tailor and tell him

" To be precise, I want the hem of this trouser folded twice".
You can as well say
"I want exactly two folds at the hem of this trouser".

All these statements are correct and relay the same message. Precise and exact all mean the same thing but you did not want to repeat yourself in both the statements.

Avoid redundancy

In your choice of words, avoid words that are useless. You know very well the words are not so meaningful or useful but you add them to your speech anyway. This drives the wrong messages sometimes. The audience might think you did not do your research well that is why you are using less useful. It also [portrays that you do not have confidence with whatever you are selling out to the people. There I nothing as bad as when the audience will think that you are not interested in what you are telling them, it will become chaotic. Therefore, it is good to avoid redundancies in your choice of words.

Importance of Words Choice

Use of incorrect words may not deliver the message

If you are addressing an audience and your words are incorrect, the crowd will hang you for them. The audience does not think of what you wanted to say, they think of what you said that is why your crucifixion or praise comes after your speech. The incorrect choice of words sends a different message thus it is very important to choose your words correctly before speaking or written or even when thinking.

Cause of misunderstanding

Incorrect word choice will cause misunderstanding. Your intention might be good but your words are not well chosen. Just like in the projects. Good projects fail due to the wrong choice of words. Companies lose a lot of money because of the wrong choice of words. The audience will misunderstand you if you choose your words incorrectly and this might result in problems.

Senselessness

You do not want to look senseless before an audience; this is so humiliating and shameful. The choice of words will make you appear sense full or senseless. The sense will come in when your choice of words is good and vice-versa will result in the senselessness. Imagine going to a podium to make a speech about the importance of unity and everyone is looking at you like you just landed from Jupiter and start shooting questions from all sides. This will freak you out and if you are not strong enough, you must just run out of the building. Your choice of words matters here.

Impact increase on mind

When you choose the correct words, the impact of the message in the mind of an audience is increased. A correct choice of words makes the audience understand better and want to know more about what you are saying or writing. You being a business who wants to add a price to your goods whereby the addition of this price will bring more money to the shareholders and better quality to the consumers. While addressing either of these groups, you decide to choose your words correctly and carefully. This idea will be appreciated and implemented not because you took a lot of time explaining and convincing them, but because you chose your words correctly and the impact of the correctness sunk the message to their minds clearly without alterations.

Your choice of words reveals your attitude and personality

Attitude is the only word that has alphabets that reach up to 100. When denoted in percentage form, this only means attitude is the only thing that can make you reach your highest potential or remain where you are. If you want positive results, you must have a positive attitude. A high level of attitude awareness should be realized by everyone and the choices of every word we say show which attitude we are harboring. If you are addressing an audience about how to prevent HIV/AIDS and your words seem not to care about the eradication, this only means, you have an attitude towards people suffering from this virus and you do not care about it. This only shows you might be giving this speech because of hidden motive which could be money, fame or anything else. Your personality is portrayed by every word you say in the speech.

We should be able to do some self-coaching in our choice of words so as not to spread nit to the audience. Before addressing an audience, you should always discover your motives. Do a self-motivation. Make yourself part of the issue you want to address, visualize the issue at hand, how the people will think and how they will see you as you address the issue. Do an internal dialogue and this will help you choose your words carefully and correctly. The words are chosen here and the attitude signified will help drive the point home safely or will cause destruction, so be careful what attitude you are showing when you speak or write.

CONCLUSION

The downfall or uprise of anything or anyone depends on the words we use. A good choice of words will do marvelous things while the wrong choice will cause pain. How your attitude is seen in your speech entirely depends on your choice of words. You might not like something, but your choice of words will say differently. Our choice of words will have to also depend on the audience we will be addressing. Controversial issues like religions have to be handled keenly with high expertise of word choices because a single match stick here can burn the entire universe. If words have always failed you and brought more chaos than good, you can always learn. Nobody was born knowing the words, we all learned these words but how we use them is entirely our choice. So, you can learn ways on how to improve on the choice of words that you use. Choice of words are like ticking time bombs, it either you detonate the bomb or you let it go off and become a calamity.

Chapter 2: Anxiety: The Worry about Other People's Thoughts about Us

It is for our own good when reality occasionally punches us in the face. And that can be through our own selves or through others. Most of us have heard that the many troubles we fear never actually get to happen. Have you really considered whether what you think others regard you to be is actually what they think of you? Oftentimes we overestimate how much and how badly people think of our failings. Many people have in this way over-inhibited themselves and they live lives far less spontaneous and less joyous than it ought to be for them.

The one thing you do or don't do because of how you expect other people to react; you need to analyze it and decide upon it in a rational manner. You surely know that you are not being true to yourself caring about others' thoughts and not your own concerning you, right? But stop and think. If you were on your deathbed this very minute, would it matter what you are worrying yourself about? I will tell you, mostly no. Think about that. Have you loved enough by now? Have you done all the things you ever wanted done by now?

True. Our happiness does depend on the quality of relationships that we keep. In fact, quite many of our routine activities involve other people. We eat with others. We socialize with others. We work with others. And we do not want to do these things with cynical people or sadists. But we are not going to peg our success or lack of it entirely on other people's expectations. You must choose to follow your heart and stop so much caring what everyone thinks. You will be amazed how life will get significantly better for you.

Worrying About Things That Won't Matter To You Later

Many do not consider it in this way. Or they just do not realize this. There are also many who despite this realization just do not know how to get started out of their already worsening situations. Worrying and fearing is the most impractical way anyone can spend their time and energy. When you worry and worry about something you want, it does not in any way become evident you will have it. Similarly, worrying about what you do not want will not get it out of your way.

Worrying is counterproductive instead. It just does not serve you. So what things are people thinking about your lack and you're buying on that to perpetuate your inaction? They are not real. Rather, inaction leads to anxiety and it overwhelms. You render yourself into a state of endless confusion and therein waste away your potentials. Watch your minds. Are they wired for negativity, only seeing difficulties and impossibilities? Undoubtedly, that is not what matters to you.

If you ever worry about anything, see it as an opportunity for you to dig deep into yourself because therein is your being and power thereof. It only matters what you make of yourself and what you use it for.

Do You Not Feel Whole Without The Approval Of Others?

Peace is found within; do not seek it without. What will you find outside that will fill a gap within you? Only you can fill your inside from inside. Choose to affect the environment. Do not wait to be affected. Affecting is the only effective way. To be affected is to be infected. You do not want that because it makes you unhealthy and ineffective, however you perceive it.

Dependence on the externalities can be the addictive cycle that will turn you away from yourself. You stand against your own chances and grounds. You rob yourself of authenticity and power. Contrary to your expectation, you drain yourself dry without recompense. What you create out of weak thoughts never holds your water. Not even for yourself or others. You become a fake. And when you become all aware, everyone turns against you because they think you lost your values.

Understand it thus; dwelling on the thoughts of others is disempowering you.

Be Content with Who You Are

Live your life for you. Have you created an ideal in your mind as a result of your mindfulness of others' thoughts? Forget it. Live your life not for others but for you. That is the right and most fitting thing to do. What you have is what you need to start with. Where you are is where you must start. How you are is all the arrangement necessary for you to embark. Any other standards you draw must be founded on these factual understandings of self.

Have you taken the time to discover yourself? That is the incredible person you must show to the world. If anyone shall matter to you, they must choose to love and admire you for who you are. Shun hanging judging yourself on the basis of those who you are trying to be. What are your values? What is your belief? What is your purpose? You need to come to the full knowledge that you are different in every way. That is how differently powerful you are. First, take care what you think about yourself. The others' thoughts come subsequent but might as well be left to be just that – their own for them.

Worrying About Others' Thoughts Doesn't Contribute to Your Positive Transformation

The person who chooses and really sees you even when you are fumbling with issues is the one who matters to you. You are obliged to live a life you are proud of, know yourself and share that with your loved ones. Stand up and advocate for yourself. Do not give that power to someone else.

Your mind will occasionally try to wander into the thoughts of others about you. Teach yourself to realize that promptly and bring it right on back to you. Whatever voids there are, fill them with your love. Stand in your own power. Show the world who you really are. And do it unapologetically. It does not matter whether or not they get to notice it.

At the end of the day, you reflect someone's image. Would you mirror the wrecked image of someone or would you be the best version of you? Be your own biggest fan.

Chapter 3: The Magical Power of Words

Magical power of words in our lives; a single word can change the emotional intensity of a message.

The magical power of words in our lives; a single word is able to change the emotional intensity of a message.

When we look beyond the religious connotations of" in the beginning there was a word", everything truly begins with a word. This word carries vibrations and sounds that they send to our minds to make the mind choose and decide whether to believe it as true or false. The reality which surrounds us is created by the vibrations consisted of the words. Words can be called as the creator, without a word, there is no reality in the thought at all. They can create a universe in your mind, they can create our lives to be able to move or remain where you are, and they can create reality.

We can always create anything we want with the words in our lives. The emotions attached to them are surprised at what they can do. From our own words, we have the most important tools that create reality. Our words provide the confirmation that lies deep within us. When someone speaks something, it is not that it just popped out of his mouth; he is confirming the reality that is in him. It is his powerful affirmation of words that his thoughts are coming into reality by speaking them to the audience.

Words are like magic; they are the labels given to emotions and feelings. The words are descriptions of your experiences. They help you understand your life. Words do not describe reality; they describe how you understand as reality. Reality is understood as perceived. Your perception of something is what your reality becomes. In simpler words, the interpretation you make of things that happen, are the words you use.

Words just like magic have the power to influence. You are always emotionally influenced by the words you read, you hear or you speak. The influence of these words may change the emotional intensity of the message by either under-delivering, over-delivering or not delivering at all. When we feel so down or lively at times, this is influenced by the words we use to describe our experiences. The intensity of the words we use either pulls us down the drain or lifts us up the clouds. You will feel good or bad according to the label; you give yourself or anything.

Words with their magical power can transform your state of mind and not only that, but they can transform your life as a whole. The words you use carries different weight to your emotional wellbeing. Your thoughts will always imp-act what you do or manifest in your life. If you say, you are going to make it in life you surely are going to make nit because you have made up your mind to work towards your goal.

Our behaviors are shaped because of the words we use. The words we use have different meanings and carry different intensity at any given time. The choice of words at any point can transform your emotions and shape your destiny. Take, for instance, political leaders. Political leaders come up with their manifestos and sell them to us using the power of words, they do it affectionately ion that we are emotionally attached to every single word they say and we end up voting them in. Some political leaders when they open their mouths to speak, they speak so well but then one word, just one lets them down. It could be a specification term or a generalization term. The intensity that term that he uses drives fear, anger, confusion and so many other mixed reactions that the audience does not want to hear him speak again. The audience starts seeing the political leader as an ill cultured person because they feel their emotions were stepped onto.

The words that we use in our daily lives carry a lot of weight. The weight the words carry can affect you or the audience emotionally. How words are expressed or said might bring a lot of chaos or a lot of joy. They can result in emotional reactions like anger, hatred, stress, frustrations and so many other reactions. Like a matchstick, the way it is so small can cause a lot of disasters buy burning down everything or it can cause a lot of joy by lighting a candle in the dark house when light is needed. This is no different from words. A single word spoken, with the intensity it carries can bring many mixed reactions that cause emotional torment or it can bring a lot of joy to the heart.

Each time we speak, we should be keen and fast to weigh the words we let go out of our mouths because you never know the impact of those words. For example, if you are in a densely crowded place, then you shout 'fire'. There will be mixed reactions. Some people will panic and start running in any of the directions while others will be so confused not to know what they can do and, in that state, they are likely to do things that are harmful because of the emotional confusion. The intensity of the word 'fire' is so strong to create a lot of emotional imbalance in the minds of the people.

The energy that words carry gives the language its capability and possibility to hurt or heal. If you could remember the first time, or anytime someone said something to you and it refused to leave your mind. It literally stuck in your mind; these only means words have weight. The emotional intensity of the message is completely changed by the weight of the words you received. For example, you go to a hospital when you are sick after the doctor runs some tests on you, he comes back with the results and tells 'you have leukemia' this might be the unprofessional way of relaying a message, but the message is correct. However, the weight of the words of the doctor will send a different message to the mind that will cause emotional problems. The emotional intensity of the message has been changed with the way the doctor said the words. The first thing after receiving that message is you die. No matter how you try to shake off the idea but it will play in your mind for quite some time or maybe forever. All this is a reminder to us that words are 'alive' they carry consciousness and we should be very conscious of how much weight they carry while using them.

When we are conscious of how to use the words bearing in mind the weight of these words, we always deepen the relationship between the words and us. We are able to understand that words not only interpret something or convey a message but they also convey feelings. We have to be able to feel the weight of every word that we speak. We have to understand that words do not exist independently, they cannot support themselves alone and they are not abstract. This means we have to know that words are the most powerful transmitters of feelings.

You may want to make an observation of how your words affect others when you speak or how other people's words affect you emotionally when they speak. You will realize that for every spoken word, there is an emotional reaction attached to it. In words, there is no single word that one can assume and call an insignificant word. Every word spoken has an emotional attachment to it and can change the message delivered. In some cases, people speak words and told to repeat they say 'never mind'. This never minds actually should be minded. The words heard while you were speaking carried weight that drove a certain reaction to the mind of your audience and you should be very mindful of this. You may realize that people who speak faster without thinking, they just throw words anyhow do not have the word power as the people who speak slowly and confidently. Those who speak confidently and slowly wield all the power of the words. The people listening to him will be keen on what he is saying. The words in his speech carry a certain weight that sinks in the mind of people well. The emotional intensity attached to the message is well received and unaltered from the slow confident speakers than the fast-careless speaker. When you become a good listener before you speak your mind, your words carry more integrity than when you rush to speak without listening. You will achieve the power of speech when you center yourself before speaking. Each time we measure the emotional intensity of our words before we speak, it will help us be intelligent message conveyers for healing messages and be able to transmit positive feelings deeply to the audience listening to us.

The words that we use have a biochemical effect on our bodies. For instance, you use the word 'terribly disappointed instead of using the word a little bit disappointed. The word terribly sends certain biochemical manufacture in our bodies that in the end causes the emotional problem. You can imagine while speaking to your sibling an argument arises arise and he tells you,' you are dumb'. This will crumble you emotionally because of the words he has used, but what if he had used words like, 'please let me explain to you how it is or let us check it up and get the real picture of the issue?' It sounds better right? This process also happens with words we use internally. When we criticize ourselves and say mean things about ourselves the biochemical effect is released.

Sometimes it causes different emotional reactions and fears just happen to be one of the emotional reactions caused by the emotional intensity of the words.

Repetitive words can carry a lot of weight in the messages. Language is learned by repeating some words almost every day. When a child is born, he does not know when to speak, but when he hears a certain word more times than the other words, he will definitely speak that word. When words are repeated most of the time, they carry a weight that affects the emotional intensity of the message. When you constantly tell yourself that, you are too fat or too thin or too ugly all the time, these words drive a message to the emotions. These words get stuck in your mind because of their repetition and they send a certain signal that activates the emotional reactions. Just like in the nursery school when we use to sing the rhymes 'row row row your boat', probably the rhyme still lingers in your mind up to now because of its repetitive nature. Each time you remember this rhyme, a certain emotional feeling is attached to it. The emotional intensity in the song makes you feel differently emotionally.

While using words, a single effective word can dampen the emotions of someone or alleviate it and they can completely change the meaning of the message. Words that affect people can cause positive effects or negative effects on the emotions of the audience. Angry words are affective words and they can send an alarm to the brains, which block the logic and all the reasoning centers from working effectively leaving one emotionally bruised. Using the right words and measuring the weight of the words we use can transform our reality and helps the emotional messages be relayed or conveyed accordingly.

Hostile words can change the emotional intensity of the message. They can disrupt certain genes that produce chemicals that keep us from stress. When these genes are disrupted, we become emotionally naked and any form of emotional disturbance hits our emotions so hard that we may not be able to withstand at times.

Some single words can increase the activity in the fear center of the brain because of the weight they impart on the emotional intensity of the message passed across. When these words increase the activity in the amygdala, which is the center fear of the brain, a lot of stress, is released which produces a chemical that interferes with the normal functioning of our brains.

Positive words or a single positive word is able to intensely affect the emotional meaning of a message. Positive words are like an airborne disease. They spread through the mind if you keep telling yourself about positive things. You will find that when positive words start spreading in your mind, your perception of different things and yourself change. You will realize that the perception of others about your changes too.

The positive use of words and the positive view of yourself help you see the good in others. If you are emotionally satisfied by what you have heard, written, or read, this means your emotions are healthy and you will feel good about them. When you feel good about yourself, you are more likely to feel good about others. An emotionally haunted person cannot regard others as good. He will always see the negative side of other people. He will always picture someone as doubtful and will constantly suspect people. This person is full of doubt and suspicion. This haunt can only be caused by emotional intensity delivered by words in the message.

We should always sit down and reflect on the harm or on the benefit a word will cause emotionally to the audience before speaking it. Reflecting on words is a process that includes one paraphrasing and stating again the words of the speaker as well as the feelings of the speaker. Be in the shoe of the audience, listen to yourself and know the emotional intensity attached to the message to be delivered. Reflecting on words you as speaker uses will help you be able to understand the emotions attached to them. It will help you have a greater understanding of the meaning of words and the feeling of those words.

Reflecting on your words before uttering helps, you hear your own thoughts. It will help you be in the shoe of the listener and be able to focus on what you will be saying and feeling. Mostly in the content, the speaker uses "you' instead of 'I". He may say "you feel terrible about the idea' instead of" I feel terrible about the idea". Reflection helps him focus and understand that he is not only addressing and conserving his emotional well being, but his words are addressing the emotional well being of the audience and the message should be passed across emotionally clear without hurting anyone emotionally. When you feel what you are saying, this will help you adjust the emotional intensity degree of every word you will use in your speech.

Reflecting on your words helps you tell the audience through your emotions that you are part of their world. If you are addressing a concern like a drought, you have to weigh the strength of the emotional impact your words will make on those affected by the drought. Your words should be able to make them emotionally comfortable and satisfied that you are standing with them during this hour of need.

When we do a reflection of our words, it helps us continue talking while motioning the emotional trigger of the audience. One is able to understand if the mood of the audience has changed during the reflection and can quickly umbrella the situation before it gets out of hand.

As much as you need to reflect on the feelings and emotions of what you are speaking, you also need to reflect on the degree of intensity of these emotions. Being emotional or reflecting on them is not bad, but is your reflection on these emotions appropriate? This is a question you should ask yourself while reflecting. Therefore, when you reflect on your words, you are required to combine both the content and the feeling to truly get the meaning of what you want to say.

Reflection of Words Before We Speak Is Based On the Two Techniques Below;

Mirroring technique

This technique is very simple and does not take much of your time. It involves one repeating keyword or the last words spoken during the reflection. One has to point out the keywords in the speech and repeat them to see the degree of intensity of emotions attached to the message. In as much as mirroring is a good technique during reflection time, make sure you do not overdo it because it will become irritating and cause a distraction from the message.

Paraphrasing technique

This is where other words are used to replace the speaker's words but the meaning is maintained. Most people have formed the mind of what they want to hear or write at a given time. It is advisable to keep away your ideas during paraphrasing and do it without bias or judgment. Paraphrasing should be non-directive.

Benefits of Watching the Degree of Intensity of the Words

Since the degree of intensity of words determines the emotional reactions of an audience, it is important to understand this and be able to remedy our failure. Below are the benefits of doing so;

Reduce the risk of hurt

When we apply the right words with the right words to our speeches, the risk of emotional hurt by the words is eliminated or reduced. Stress, confusion and many more mixed reactions arising from the degree of intensity of the message will be elevated if not at all reduced.

Certainty

Words well chosen with the correct intensity have certainty that gives hope to the emotionally deranged. Imagine giving a speech of help to the hunger-stricken families somewhere in the world, your weight of words will show the certainty in the speech and will restore hope to the victims.

Eliminates misinterpretation

One single word can change the entire message. The weight this word carries sends a different message emotionally to the receiver. If we can be able to choose our words well with the appropriate weight they deserve, we will be able to eliminate the misinterpretation of the message.

Shows the attitude accorded

Attitude is a very important thing while using words. Your attitude defines your habits which defines your behavior. The words you choose with their respective weight shows or reveals your attitude to the audience. One is able to understand or know that you are with them in whatever the issue and you like being with them or not at all. Your attitude while addressing the audience will drive the emotional harm or health to the mind of the audience.

CONCLUSION

The emotional intensity of any message is determined or characterized by the words we say. Words can change meaning because of the weight they carry. You may want to pass a certain message across but due to the degree of intensity of the words you are using the message will be distorted. It will not be a clear message and it can be misquoted.

Each time you open your mouth to speak, put in mind the impact your words will make on the audience. Is it a negative or positive impact? The positivity or negativity of the words in your speech is brought about by the weight the words hold. You have to be careful with some words for they carry the weight that can cause more irreparable damage.

Words cannot be called back once spoken but a remedy can be applied to ease the pain, hurt or ruin they caused. You have to put in mind that some words are more disastrous than others because of the weight they cause. For example, if you hear the word " death" and "sick", what comes to your mind first? It is sadness. Both death and sick are saddening words but the degree of intensity each word carry is different from each other. The word death is more saddening than the word sick because of the weight accorded to it. In death, there is no hope and in sickness, there is hope that he will be well.

Therefore, the degree of intensity of any word is always formed by our minds and then the mind attaches different emotions to the words. This is simply notifying us that words come into reality when we ourselves define reality. How we define ourselves in the mind is how our reality comes into being.

Mark this, each time you speak, the audience filters the words that you have used basing on their psycho-emotional state. During this filtering, they can interpret the meaning of these words wrongly. That is why it is very important for you to know that one single word spoken or written by you can easily change the emotional intensity of a message.

Chapter 4: Power of Words in Strengthening, Encouraging and Boosting Confidence

The words we use also have power over our lives; Words help us improve others-encourages and strengthens your self-esteem and that of others.

Words can make a difference in our lives and in the lives of others. The real power in our lives is in the words we speak as much as thoughts impact what we manifest. Our words confirm our most internal thoughts. The sub-consciousness of any person is always awoken or represented by the words the person speaks.

The words we speak to ourselves or to others are like a lamp that gives light. This lamp lights your path so as to be able to see clearly the direction you are heading to and be able to fulfill your goal and objectives. If we allow well-lit paths that the words provide in our lives, this will transform us into better humans that will be able to know the direction of life and understand completely where we are supposed to head.

When you open up your mouth to speak or when you decide to write at any given time, always put in mind that you are either going to encourage yourself or pull yourself down, the speech you will make will define who you are, also mind that you are going to encourage someone or hurt someone by taking away what would have made him better. Make sure that you always have something good to say.

Speaking good things are likely to encourage you or the person you are talking to. When your words are good, they are likely to bring the best out of you and out of your audience. You must also make sure you have the knowledge of what you are talking about. Good knowledge of your facts or ideas is able to instill confidence in you or your audience. If you have ever known the answer in the class and then the teacher points to you to give out the answer, you feel so confident when giving out your answer because you are certain that it is the correct answer. This is the same with words. Have full knowledge of what you are saying so that your words can encourage you and the audience you are addressing.

Sometimes no matter how much you have tried to improve yourself and others by encouraging them and strengthening their self-esteem you find that your efforts hit a rock. Your efforts are just simply not fruitful at all and this dampens you completely. There is always a way for everything. Even the most strongly built walls have a loophole of bringing them down. Same to your situation, there is a way that can make you be able to reach the hearts and minds of people through the words you speak.

First, consider the "If's' that makes life worthwhile

Life is worthwhile if you learn

Words shape our lives in one way or the other. This means we have to always learn the words that can improve the self-esteem of others and encourage them. If you do not know anything in life the best weapon to know it is by leaning. If life is worthwhile while we learn, good encouraging words can be obtained by learning too.

Life Is Worthwhile If We Learn From Our Own Experience.

They say experience is the best teacher. Our experiences are defined by the words we speak and these experiences will help you be able to encourage someone and strengthen their self-esteem. The positive or negative experiences in your life can be used as a weapon through your words to encourage someone. If at a certain point in life you failed, your experience about this failure can be used to encourage someone to pursue his or her goals through the words you speak.

Life is worthwhile if we learn from others

Learning from others is the best way to understand something. Sometimes you may learn something but later on find out that you do not the thing you learned about, it is fine, but words of encouragement, strengthening words can be learned from others. They could be motivational speakers or experts in the fields. When you learn what others are saying to encourage people, you will be able to encourage someone through your words too.

Life is worthwhile if we try

In life you do not give up, you do not stay wherever you are and wait for your judgment. You must do something to improve your situation. This is not any different from words. You cannot give up because your words are not encouraging and no one seems to like everything that comes out of your mouth. You must fight. Try again and again and again until you make it. They say winners never quit, and if they quit, they have won. Therefore, with words, for you to be able to strengthen someone or even yourself, try as many times as possible.

Life is worthwhile when we are selective

If you want to go far in life, have goals. Select them one by one. Have priorities and you will know what you want. In the case of words, it is the same. If you want encouraging words, esteem strengthening words, be selective. You cannot just go out there and say everything that pops up in your mind. Choose what to say every time. Words are as if the lamp is shown direction. If you cannot select them carefully, you might not just get enough light to light your path.

The "Ifs" of life will help you improve and know how to use your words to encourage others and even yourself. Each time we speak, we should always put in mind that words once said they never are forgotten even if they can be forgiven. Sometimes we may not even want to say some words but our tongues are like beasts that are constantly trying to get out their cages, it is only that if we let some beasts out that they will cause grief to us and to everyone else listening to us.

The tongue has no bones but it can break so many hearts including yours. We should put in mind that each time we speak; one kind word can change someone's whole day or even life. There are other fragile minds that just need encouragement and kindness. They need someone to utter kind words to encourage them or uplift their self-esteem. As a speaker, your words should be able to do this. The echoes of kind words are longer and stronger. They are soothing, encouraging and strengthening to anyone. They should be kind enough to change someone's life and days positively.

The words we say to people and to ourselves change our worlds and their world completely. They are like seeds that do not just land anywhere but in the hearts. We have to be careful what we planting by the words we say because we might just one day eat the produce of what we planted. We have seen political instabilities in countries, wars in those countries, the leaders and citizens of those countries just need some words of encouragement, words that will lift their confidence to keep on hoping for better, but if we go there and plant different seeds, seeds that are not worthwhile, they will grow in the hearts of those people and they will not only bring problems to them but to you as well.

Always make sure that you do not mix your bad moods with your words. Your bad moods will always influence your words negatively and this will be discouraging to you and your audience. Your bad moods should always be handled separately from your words because moods can be changed with time but you will never get any chance to replace the bad words that you say. Broken bones can always heal faster but wounds that words open will never heal. They will be permanent in your heart and mind and might continue discouraging someone as each day goes by.

If we want to under5stand the power of our thoughts, we, first, have to understand the power of our words. If we understand what words can do to the lives of others rather than encouraging them and strengthening their self-esteem, we would simply decide to be silent forever when it comes to anything that is negative. We always create our own weaknesses and strengths in our thoughts and words. We always have a choice to replace the negative with the positive when we talk to encourage and boost self-esteem.

How Your Words Can Affect Your Life

Words can encourage you, strengthen your self-esteem or discourage you. When you say negative things like " I cannot, I am a loser, I am a total failure, I will try", your subconscious interprets these words because our subconscious interprets what it hears. In the end, our bodies and minds follow the lead of leads. The words we utter act as direction to what we do.

To achieve confidence, influence, connection and other encouraging and strengthening things, start with what you say to the audience each time you stand up to give a speech. Speeches have powers; they start as words and in the end, turns into deeds.

The words you use against yourself hold a lot of power. The power that will give you confidence and the strength to move on or the power to make you feel inadequate and feeble, the power to bring forth opportunities in your life each time you say them or the power to take away those opportunities.

Using negative words in your life will hold you down and you will not be able to rise beyond your reality. Just like a house, we live in words that are the same as a house. The words you will speak to yourself is like your own house. If you do not sweep or clean your house it will become so dirty that no one will want to come near it. If you do not do anything about your negative words, they will continue pressing you down that you will be lost in them. Words like 'never, am doomed' will never give you an opportunity to build your skills in anything.

The world looks at you and defines through the words that you use. Your words are your own mirror that gives a reflection of who you are. When you use negative words about yourself, it will be very hard for you to stand up to your challenges and meet your goals. The negative words you say about your self-drives in pessimism, fear, anxiety and so many other dreadful things that in the end shapes your reality. When you use positive words about yourself, this will help you be able to keep on fighting and have a clear sight of your goals and what is required of you.

You should be able to develop positive thinking habits that will help you be able to think positively about yourself. The habits that will help shape your reality into positivity. Below are some habits that will help you be able to embrace the goodness in you and lead to a positive strengthening of your self-esteem.

Spend your time with positive people

When you spend your time with negative people, their negativity is likely to transfer itself to you. Words are learned by the repetitive strategy so if you hang out with the negatively worded people, they will make you start thinking negatively and you will give out negative words, which will not encourage you. If you sp[end your time with the positive people, they could be friends, family members, their positivity will transfer to you which will fix your thinking and change the words that come out of your mouth from the draining ones to the strengthening ones.

Be responsible for your behavior.

In life when you encounter problems and difficulties, stand up to them and own them up. Do not go about whining and blaming people for what is happening in your life. Accepting your responsibilities in the problems and difficulties will help you learn from them and be able to prevent them in the future. The experiences you go through while handling these problems are the ones that will help you use the right words to encourage someone, strengthen their self-esteem, and encourage yourself.

Help

Be a contributor to the community. Your contributions through words that encourage are able to also shape your life positively. They will encourage you and lift your self-esteem. If you have ever helped anyone and then received that "thank you" word, it elevated your esteem to a different level. It makes you want more "thank you" because you feel good. Helping gives you a new view of the world and helps in your positive thinking.

You should read inspirational and positive materials

We have said that positivity or negativity is communicable. It spreads from one person to another. When you read positive materials, you are more likely to fix your thinking into positive thinking. You will be inspired by the positivity of the materials and thus try to think in the same way as the writers of the materials. The materials will leave you more confident, more motivated and more competent. The positivity influenced by the positive and inspirational materials will help you use good words or positive words about yourself.

Point out and replace the negative thoughts.

To be successful you must make sure that negative thoughts are not hanging above your head like a dark cloud. If the negative thoughts are above, it could rain any time which will not be good for you or your audience. Make sure that you recognize all the negative thoughts and replace them with positive thoughts. The positive thoughts will help build your self-esteem and confidence.

Consider negativity consequences.

In life, everything we do has consequences. In every speech we make there are consequences. All the words we use against or for ourselves have consequences. Words bring about deeds, so you should think about the consequence of every word. Is it going to encourage you or discourage you? You should understand the consequences if you think negative about yourself and if you think positive about yourself. You will realize that negative thinking will bring a lot of harm to you. After knowing this, it is better that you adjust your thinking band change from negativity to positivity.

Take care of yourself

Self-care will help you be able to think positively. Getting enough rest, exercising, and eating well helps release and reduce stress. It lightens up your moods and when your moods are good the words you think about yourself are good too. The mental and physical health maintained it would help you think positively about yourself.

Have your own daily gratitude list

Keeping a record of your accomplishments daily will keep your mind positive. It will encourage you to accomplish more good things and this imparts positivity in your words and deeds. This gives you more confidence and encouragement to forge ahead.

Recall your best experiences

By remembering your happy past, it gives you hope and encouragement when talking about yourself or when judging yourself. Your happy past will flashlight of positivity into your thinking and you will realize that things are not as bad as you think. It will make you realize that you can do anything you want to do. You can be able to say the right words about yourself as you want.

Do what you like

Doing what you like gives you a lot of positivity. The words you will use about yourself will be filled with positivity because this is something you really like. It is just like forcing your child to do something they do not like. They will feel hated, they will useless, they will feel hopeless unlike when the child himself decides to do their own things. They will feel so happy and even see themselves as heroes. They will speak positively about themselves and this helps shape their life around themselves and around others.

Controlling your emotions

This is something that most people are not able to master. When you control your emotions, you will be able to measure what you say about you. If you are angry and mood, this does not mean that you are a failure, it only means that you are feeling bad and you will come out of it. If you let, your emotions define your words, your words will define you and the image you will see in the mirror of words will break you more than encourage you.

The habits above will help you think positively about yourself and in the end, will make your words encourage you and strengthen yourself-esteem.

The words that we say can also be of much importance to others by encouraging them and strengthening or improving their confidence in whatever they do. To harness the power of the words we speak to others, we should:

Express gratitude.

Gratitude helps change everything. A magic word makes someone feel complimented, encouraged and confident enough to do something else for you. When you show gratitude through your words to someone, you are improving the thinking of this person and the confidence that he has. He will have the courage to do better than harm.

Offer positivity

Instead of giving a wrong compliment like "you look like a monkey with that makeup", offer another positive word. You can simply say, "please let me redo your makeup, this one does not suit you well". All the statements hold the same meaning, but the words in the first statement are negative and damaging. They are discouraging and may make someone hate themselves forever, while the words in the second statement are encouraging, they strengthen someone's confidence and makes them feel that a change of the makeup is better. The words maintain positivity, which is good.

Do not participate in negativity

When you participate in negativity, the words that will come out of your mouth will be negative and their aim will be to disco rage, cause stress and other emotional tortures. These words will drain someone of confidence and they will not want to listen to you again or if they do, they will feel lost and stuck in their own realities that will make their lives useless.

Be constructive

Construct something that will help strengthen someone's self-esteem and not bring it down. Let your words be constructive in a way that they will encourage someone and not discourage them. Words have more power than the most fearful bombs so you have to be very careful and constructive while using them to be able to achieve your goals of encouragement.

You Should Offer Compliments to Others

Your words of compliments encourage people. Any compliment offered to drive all the way to the mind and to the heart. When someone is complimented, his confidence kicks in and he is able to positively do other good things that will shape his life the life of others. Each time you offer a compliment by your words, just know that you are touching hearts and mind minds of more than just the audience. As much as a bad word is like a wildfire, a good word lasts and builds. On a morning at the office, just complimenting someone's good dressing is enough to put a smile on the face of that person. Maybe that person had a rough night or morning, but you have been able to encourage him to push through the day by complimenting him. Your compliment to him is like holding his hand when he was stuck, pulling him up and telling him, you can do it.

Summarily, the words we speak to ourselves and others either encourage us or discourages us. We can always increase or decrease our own happiness by choosing to speak the right words to ourselves. We can upset others or ourselves by also speaking unnecessarily about things that hurt us or have hurt us.

When you speak optimism to yourself or another person, optimism follows, you band him or her. If you speak negative things, negativity follows you. The interpretation of our reality is in our words, so if you use your words without knowing the impact, they will create a reality that you may not like or others may not like and will end up bringing harm.

Habits that help your positive thinking helps you get the right words to use. Words that boost confidence, words that strengthen the self-esteem of others, words that encourage others are all gotten from the habits we have. When our habits portray a lot of negativity, our words will mostly be negative, positive habits will give positive encouraging words.

Words may seem so small and tinny but what they do in our lives is wondrous, so be careful when speaking, think first before you speak. You might be discouraging rather than encouraging.

Chapter 5: Words Shape the Beliefs, Values, and Destiny of a Person

Language is something we learn from the environment in which we live and varies according to location, culture, and religion.

The words we use to interpret our reality. This means our reality is what constitutes our beliefs, our values, and our destiny. Words used when speaking form, a language pattern, which is a means of communication. The language we speak influences how we see the world. How we look at the world, how we see things is the manifestation of the words that we use in our languages. The principle of linguistic relativity states that the language people use to describe or discuss the world directly influences the way people think about the world. Every time we use words, we have to be careful because they hold our destinies and not just that but words can hurt just as much as any physical pain inflicted on you by someone.

A word that you use in your daily life is able to shape the way you think or the way you judge life. The words can shape your values. The values of a person are motivated by actions or attitudes. The words you use are also motivated by actions or attitudes. The actions you take when speaking are very important in your speech. If you feel that you have gone wrong or your words have been misquoted, it is better to take an action and own up the responsibility of clearing up the confusion.

The values we uphold in life are always described by the words we use. Good values that bring about positivity and prosperity in people's lives are shaped by the words we say or write. If we write or speak positivity, that will be a stepping stone of our values. The negativity in the values is also shaped by the words we speak. If you speak negativity, you are planting it and anything that is planted where there are favoring conditions must grow. The negativity will grow and shape our values in that manner. Our attitude as a value contributes to everything in our lives.

The attitude we develop will always come from the words we say to ourselves or the words that we are told by others. Since the words said are an expression of our realities, attitude as a value is shaped by this world and it either contributes negatively or positively to our realities. The attitude value that the shape of the word is able to shape our destinies. One's destinies can be determined by the attitude he has. If words shape values, those values will help the words shape our destinies.

The words and language we use to describe our experiences whether bad or good, holds a lot of power in shaping our view of the world. The words we use help us express our values and our ideas. They help us be able to refer to our attitudes and they end up shaping our behaviors. When our behaviors are shaped, our beliefs are shaped too by these very words. For example, when you tell your child every day that he is so dumb and failure, each time he sits he will remember these words and he will behave in a dump way and also in a way that failures behave. You will find that this child will believe within no time that he is not good at anything because you as a parent told him so. He will not be able to accomplish anything because he believes that he does not know anything and he will fail because he is a failure.

The greater good of something that you believe in is always shaped by the words you tell yourself and believe. Our own destinies are determined or shaped by our very own words. Since words interpret our realities, our realities can interpret our destinies. What we think of or do is all because of words. When we want to do something, we cannot do that thing without using words to describe or interpret what we want to do. If we want to communicate to our audience more effectively, we must use words. Even graphical communications will need words to be well understood.

What other think of you can only be described through words? If others think that you are good, intelligent, beautiful, all these can only be done through words. Look at the sign language, with all the beauty it holds, if you know sign language and someone tells you in sign language that you are beautiful, it won't feel as good as when someone used words to describe how beautiful you are. You will want to hear every single detail of how beautiful you are and this cannot be achieved in any other means rather than in words.

What we tell ourselves, we do so through words. When we talk to ourselves, whether negatively or positively we are only able to do so through the words we use. If you want to tell yourself that you are a conqueror, you are only able to do that through words. The word conquer is a word that will help you reach your destiny. It shapes the destiny you will go through your thinking.

How we remember those that we loved so much and died or left us can only be done through words. Our experiences, grievances, fears, anxiety, pain is only achieved through words. Someone is able to know that you are grieving or you are happy through words. Your way of speaking is expressed by the words, which interpret the reality of the moment.

How we explain our future, we are only able to so by use of the words. Our futures are our destinies. These destinies are shaped by the words we speak. When explaining to someone how you want to settle in a certain country in the future, how you want to buy a certain model of a car within a certain time, all these are done through words. Nobody will understand how your future is planned if you simply keep quiet and look at them, It is either you write it down or speak it out from your mouth for one to know, and all these will be done by the use of words.

We imagine the perfection of things and use our words to explain this perfection. We bring it out and so lively that it is the only reality we have and see. When someone says she carries the epitome of beauty. The word epitome is the perfect word, but when the words epitome beauty falls in your ears than in your mind, you will see a reality in the phrase and you will make it real.

How we describe our feelings, how we make someone smile, how we speak to our souls to heal, how we describe our dreams, all these and many others must have words attached to them so that they can make sense and bring upon reality. Do you think anything would have existed if words did not exist at all? No. Nothing will exist without words. Destinies will not be shared without words. Values will not be shaped without words and cultures will not even dare exist without the words. The words are the only intervention that gives us humans our sense of immortality. Words are the only powerful tools in human life that will determine your existence and destiny.

Language patterns are formed by words we speak. It is like a mother giving birth to a child. The words are the mother and the language is the child. There are various languages that people speak around the globe. There are different language variations and these languages can influence the beliefs, behaviors, values, thinking, and culture of people. The language variation is the characteristic of the language. There are so many ways of saying some things in different ways but maintaining the meaning of the things you are talking about. Some things like pronunciation in languages can vary, word choices can vary and grammar too can vary but the meanings of the words are maintained.

Languages can be learned from different environments, which we live in but they can vary according to location, culture, and religion.

The Causes of Difference in languages

Settlement patterns

Where we settle or live determines the language we speak. The density of the population will determine the language we speak. There is a saying that says when you go to roam, you do what the Romans do. It is not by force you speak the language of someone else, but you will find yourself speaking the language the majority of the people are speaking for ease of communication. For example, the African Americans in

Chicago, if you listen to their English language are different from the other Americans' English. They speak like they are singing without minding punctuations at all. Their sentences are sometimes longer than the time you can use to hold your breath. This does not mean their language changes the meanings of a word, it only means their pronunciations and grammar is different but the meaning of the words is maintained. Any person that goes to live in Chicago, within no time will be speaking this type of English so that he can be able to communicate easily and fit in. This kind of language is brought about by the settlement patterns.

The Migration routes

When people migrate from one place to another, a boundary of the dialect is developed and set. No other language crosses the boundary to come in. The set boundaries are to enable maintain the language the people speaking it from vanishing or mixing with another language that they cannot understand.

Language contact

This happens when during migration, people interact with different other peoples with different languages and in the process, they borrow vocabularies, pronunciation, and grammar or syntax from their languages. As a result, a language is formed due to language contact.

Geographical factors

Some languages come about because of the geography of the location of the people. Rivers, lakes, and mountains affect the movement of people hence they end up settling for one language that makes sense to all of them since the geographical factors tend to isolate them from other speakers. For example, in Africa, there is a group of people that were divided by the mountains and they called themselves the highland nilotes. All the highland nilotes speak one language in a country called Kenya in the eastern part of Africa from the other group of nilotes, the plain nilotes, and the river lake nilotes because they were separated from other speakers and could only master one language. Therefore, geographical factors cause differences in the language.

The region and occupation of people

The people in rural areas are more likely to speak a language that is outdated than the people living in urban areas. The people in the urban areas are exposed to the diversity of so many other languages while the people of the rural area only have one language that they can communicate with. This makes it a more reason of language variation.

The linguistic process

The new developments and improvement in the pronunciation and simplification of the grammar of languages give language a difference and these results in the difference in the language people speak. When the grammar is the change for simplification purposes, it changes how the words sound even though the meaning is maintained. For example, the pronunciation of the words "chips and fries" is different, even the grammar in it is different but the meaning is the same. These are Irish potatoes chopped and deep-fried in the cooking oil to give them a crunchy taste when you eat them. The development of the word chips brought about fries, and that contributed to the difference in the language.

Group -reference

Different groups of people speak different languages. Groups could be an ethnic group, a nation, age gender and even the origin of the ancestors. Different ethnic groups speak different languages that make them understand each other. Different nations have national languages or language that is different or might be same as another nation that they share some things. Age groups and age sets have their own languages. Every age has its own language. To some ages, languages are like fashions, they speak a certain language only during that age bracket but when they move to another age, they drop the language and move along with the one in the age bracket they have moved in.

Each human gender has its own language just like there is grammatical gender. A certain gender is described by the language it uses or is used against them. For example, the word "bitch" is an irritating word yes, it is normally used to refer to females provocatively. At no time whatsoever can this word be used to mean a man. While the word "men", is mostly used by African Americans to mean friend or male friend. A sentence, "I have missed you, men". This sentence means that he has missed his friend. The word men can never be used to refer to a woman at any time.

Social class

The cause of the difference in languages can be due to the difference in the social class. Different social classes speak different languages that reflect the education of the speakers and their level of income. A class of lawyers will speak their own language that they can understand as well as a group of doctors can speak their own language that is understandable to them only during their talks. Therefore, the difference in the social class is a cause of the difference in the languages.

Language and Culture

The values, beliefs, attitudes and behavioral conventions shared by a certain or specific group are what we call culture. Language and culture share a big connection. The patterns in the languages we speak give culture disposition and priorities. We cannot interact with another language without interacting with its culture. When you learn a new language, it is not all about learning its alphabets, grammar or word arrangement, it goes deeper this. You have to learn the specific society's customs and culture.

There are different cultures that have more words that mean one word. Aboriginal groups like the Pormpuraaw on the western edge of Cape York in Australia have different words that mean one word. They do not use words like left, right or center. They rely on obsolete directions for space. They keep track of where they are going or coming from or are settled even in the most unfamiliar places. The Pormpuraaw uses words like east, west, south, and north. Quite confusing, right? Yea it is. They maintain the obsoleteness for space. If you asked a person from this group, where the remote controller of the television is, he will answer you by using the direction. His answer could be, "the remote is on your southwest".

Different languages spoken by different people around the world changes how people interact with each other. There are people that are bilingual and it is believed that their thinking is different especially when they switch from one language to another. Languages just like their parent words are learned and when trying to learn a language, always bear in mind that it is very important that the culture from which you are learning that language be referenced.

When learning the languages in different cultures you will need paralanguage. Paralanguage will help transmit messages in different languages because human communication is very complicated. When you are raised in a certain society, you will automatically learn about the tones, the gestures, the glances and other communication tools that will help you put emphasis on what you are putting across.

Observation and imitating people that are close to you mostly learn these communication strategies of culture. They could be close relatives and family members then, later on, you will start learning from people that are away from your close relative. The immigrants are more likely to get difficulty in picking languages in the places they have moved to than their little children because;

The language humans speak is instinctive. Every language spoken in any culture has instincts attached to it. The older immigrants have their instincts attached to their languages from their cultures and it is very hard for them to learn a new language, unlike their children.

The language we speak is an adaptation of where we come from and evolutional. Languages just like cultures evolve. The mature immigrant's languages already evolved through their culture that is why they are finding it difficult to master the new language unlike their little children, their language is still evolving and can pick any language during their evolution of languages.

Image: words destroy self and others

The languages we speak are characteristics of science and human nature should be understood first. Understanding your nature includes understanding your culture. The immigrants will find it hard to learn the language faster because it is not in their culture. The nature of the language is different from what they know; unlike the children who will simply adapt to nature and are able to learn the language very fast.

The language we speak was developed together by the culture. These two being intertwined they influenced each other. Alfred L Kroeber, a cultural anthropologist said that "culture started when speech was available and from that beginning, the enrichment of either one led to the other to develop much further. This means without language, culture would not be there and also, culture is the consequence of the interactions of every human being and the acts of the humans' communication are just their cultural manifestations within a specific community. All the set attributes of any culture are expressed through the language.

LANGUAGE AND CULTURE

The different religions in the world just like languages evolve. The language spoken in different religions differs from each other. When you must acquire religion, then it involves learning some new vocabulary and grammar. For example, some religions like the Quakers use the word "thee" and other Christians use the words like to believe "on "Jesus instead of to believe" in "Jesus such language patterns have psychological effects on the speaker which in the end limits his thoughts.

In religions, there are different sacred languages that are used. For instance, Islam used Arabic, the Hebrews uses Judaism, and Buddhism uses Pali. Different languages are accorded to every different religion basing on their beliefs and values. The languages used by these religions have seen ages. They are archaic and remote but their remoteness is a symbol of strength and not weakness. When anyone tries to bring these remote languages up to date, it will result in the loss of faith.

The universal features in different religions provide the grammatical similarities among the languages. These results in the languages in the religions become parallel. In Christianity, there is the religion is parallel in that there are Catholicism and Protestantism. The Catholics are moiré devoted to the Virgin Mary and feel that Protestants are not, which is true, there is no single devotion to Mary in the protests because they only believe she was a vessel and devotion is accorded to her.

In Buddhism, there is a difference between Mahayana and Theravada. Theravada is unemotional while Mahayana is not. The Muslims, there are differences in the tones of Sunni and Shia.

Conclusively, the words that we speak to ourselves and to other people can always shape beliefs, values cultures or destinies. One's value is determined by the words he puts in in his mind. Your destiny is also determined by words. What you say, what you think, how you express your experiences, how you plan your future is all done by the words. Our beliefs and cultures are determined by our words and we should always be careful when using words because they can shape you the way they are being used.

We have looked at languages. It is important to understand that languages derive from words. The language patterns we use come from the words we utter. Different cultures and religions uphold different languages hence language variation. The language variations are caused by a variety of things discussed above. The languages we speak can be learned and the mastery of any language depends on the age of a person. Children are more likely to master languages faster than older people are.

Languages we use to influence different, religions, cultures, beliefs, values like attitude, behavior and even the thinking of a person. The effects of language on a person's attitude show how the person views the world. The words used in languages are able to reference the attitude of someone and shape the behavior of that person.

Chapter 6: Conversation: Developing Empathy by Improving Conversational Skills

Just about everyone engages in various forms of communication on a day to day basis. One of the most common forms of communication is through conversation. Conversation can be face to face in which the person you are able to see the person you are talking to. Similarly, conversation might also be in the form of online conversation whereby you talk to another person through various digital platforms. Despite the prevalence of conversation as a preferred mode of communication, you might end up feeling misunderstood in a conversation you are having with someone else. Similarly, the people you talk to might also feel the same way about you. This feeling can be attributed to a lack of empathetic communication.

Empathetic communication can be defined as communication that seeks to enhance empathy through conversation. Empathy in this context refers to your ability to adequately understand other people, their point of views and the idea that they are trying to put across. Ultimately, empathetic communication seeks to make it much easier for you to really understand what the person next to you is saying. You, therefore, end up being a good communicator by doing so.

Learn to listen

There are several ways through which you can develop empathy by enhancing your conversation skills with one such approach being improved listening. Many people are very good at talking but quite poor when it comes to listening. You might find that you always want to insist on having your say in a conversation but at the same time, you are not really interested in what others have to say. This is because you are a poor listener. Similarly, it is also common to appear to be listening to someone else but you are not really listening to them. If you cannot really listen to someone, then you might not be able to know exactly how they feel about the issue at hand and where exactly they are coming from.

Being a good listener is a great conversational skill that can enhance deeper understanding hence empathy. First and foremost, you will be able to hear everything that the other person has to say and their position on an issue. Enhanced listening can also enable you take notice of important aspects such as the tone of voice of the person you are having a conversation with. The tone of voice can tell you a lot about how exactly the other person feels about an issue. For instance, someone might agree to something but with a resigned tone of voice. Such a person might, therefore, agree to your idea because they feel obliged to do so. Ultimately, learning to listen more will significantly enhance your conversation skills and make you more empathetic towards others.

Do not be a selective listener

When it comes to listening, there are people who engage in what is referred to as selective listening. Selective listening refers to an activity in which you mainly end up choosing what you want to hear and not listening to everything that the other person has to say. Selective listening can be attributed to some inherent fears that a person might have regarding a particular topic and thus, they might not be open to the idea of openly discussing such a topic. Selective listening is a major hindrance when it comes to empathetic communication since you do not get to listen to everything that the other person has to say. The overall implication is that you will not be able to fully understand the concerns, the fears and the perspective that the other person has on an issue.

On the contrary, when you are able to do away with selective listening in your conversations, you will be in a better position to understand another person. You will be able to really put yourself in their position, appreciate their concerns, fears, life goals and objectives. This will improve your overall interaction with them.

Do not be prejudiced

Prejudice refers to beliefs that you might be having regarding other people or groups of people. For instance, that all Muslims are intolerant. Prejudices are most often than not regarded as pure misconceptions and they can significantly distort empathetic communication. When you are engaged in a conversation with other people and you have already made up your mind who they are, then you might not be able to see things from their perspective. They will, therefore, end up feeling misunderstood thus negating the very essence of empathetic communication.

Eliminating various forms of prejudice is a vital conversation skill that can go a long way in improving your capacity to empathize with others. You will not allow any false beliefs or misconceptions inform on your opinion of other people. Instead, you will listen to the, and come up with an informed opinion about who they are and what their aspirations might be. Such people will end up feeling that you have understood them and this will make you an empathetic communicator.

Importance of empathetic communication

You might have gone through all the aforementioned ways of improving your empathetic conversation skills but still wondering, what is the importance of empathetic communication? First and foremost, empathetic conversational skills improve your understanding of the person you are having a conversation with. A good understanding of other people is very important when it comes to your day to day interaction with them. This is because you will be able to get to know their sensitivities and thus have a good idea of what to say and what not to say while interacting with them.

Secondly, empathetic conversation and communication, in general, can also make you a much better person. You will be able to be a better friend, colleague or even spouse when you constantly engage in empathetic conversation. This is because;

enhanced understanding of other people will make you know their needs and aspirations in life. You will thus be in better position to contribute in your little way towards the realization of such needs and aspirations hence making you a better human being.

Connection with other people is an inherent human need. No one wants to lead a lonely life but this might happen if you cannot connect with others. Empathetic conversation will enable you to connect very well with the people around you and you will end up making friends from all walks of life. This implies that your life will generally be enhanced since other people will be more than willing to be around you and interact with you on a daily basis since they feel that you are able to really connect with them.

How to go about developing empathetic conversation

It is very important to know how to go about developing empathetic conversation skills. Generally, you should start with the process by enhancing the conversation that you have with those around you. It is important to connect well with those around you before you can extend the same to others. Start by listening more to your family members, your friends, and colleagues at work. Workplaces are more diverse than ever nowadays and this implies that you should not be influenced by any prejudices about some of your colleagues at work and their socio-cultural backgrounds. By doing so, you will be able to create a better pool of inner circle members who you can easily connect with.

In addition to improving the conversations that you have with those close to you, it is also important to improve the same when it comes to other people including strangers and groups. Try not to judge a person when you first encounter them. In case, you are interacting with a group of people from a specific community say Asians or Arabs, try not to allow any prejudices to crop into your mind while interacting with them. This is because; such prejudice will undermine your perception of them hence undermining the whole conversational process. All in all, improved empathetic communication at the communal level will make you a better member of society. This distinction can also come in handy in case you try to ascend to any leadership role in the community since many people would be willing to have people in authority who they can easily connect with.

To sum it all up, empathetic conversation refers to a conversation in which one is able to really understand the other person. There are various ways through which you can develop this essential conversation skills and it includes listening more to other people and what it is that they are saying. Furthermore, you should avoid selective listening since you will not be able to fully understand the perspective of the other person if you do this. As an empathetic communicator, you should also shun away from prejudice since they will undermine your capacity to understand others. Ultimately, as an empathetic communicator, you will be able to better understand others, attract other people into your life and become a better person. Finally, in order to develop your empathetic communication skills, you should first and foremost start with those around you before moving onto strangers and larger groups of people.

Chapter 7: Be Interesting: Develop the Skills Of Great Successful People

Each and every person wants to be successful at one point or the other in their lives. However, many people do not simply know how to go about attaining success. There are many drags to riches stories out there but some of them fail to capture the essence of what one needs in order to be successful. Of course, there are the obvious things that many successful people would be more than willing to point out including the fact that you should be a hard-working individual, stay focused on your dreams, letting your money work for you among others. But the truth of the matter is, your personality can go a long way in making you a success story. Simply put, the way other people perceive you can make or break your dreams. This is because; it is the people around you who will be the driving force towards your success. For instance, if you are businessman, your customers will be the key to your success. If you are a lawyer, accountant or real estate agent, your clients will be the key to your success.

One of the ways through which you can enhance your chances of attaining success is simply by being interesting. When you are an interesting person, other people would be more than willing to listen to and literally, buy into your ideas. At this point you are probably asking yourself; how do I go about being an interesting person? Do not worry, the next few paragraphs will be dedicated to answering that question.

Make others feel like they know you

We are unique in one way or the other and this implies that we all have the potential to be interesting. The main mistake is that many people make is fear letting other people know them since they think they will be misjudged. However, in order for people to find you interesting, you have to make them feel like they really know you. Obviously, you should not be an open book and reveal all your dirty little secrets to the whole world. Instead, you should allow others to know something or even several things about you that portray you in a positive light.

One of the most reliable ways that has worked for many successful people is by sharing an interesting story about yourself. The story should capture the essence of some of the values that you espouse such as hard work, resilience and even your love for humanity. For instance, you can say something about how you were brought up in a poor background where you lacked access to a square meal day in row but still managed to reach where you are. Having a background story about yourself and one that is actually interesting will make other people find you interesting and willing to be around you and work with you. However, as much as you need to make the story interesting, you should always avoid giving in to the temptation of lying. With all the technology around, one can easily dig into your past and if they find out that you are a liar, then you can kiss goodbye any dreams you ever had of being successful.

Have several interesting stories about other people

Everyone loves a story. There are millions of interesting positive stories out there that might not necessarily be in the public domain. In addition to telling other people an interesting background story about yourself, you can also make a habit of sharing the stories of other people. Find one that you know will captivate the attention of others and one that has not been popularly shared in the public domain. This is because not many people will have the time and patience for a story that they already know.

Just like is the case with your background story, the story that you select should one that seeks to promote values that you want to be identified with. Sharing interesting stories about others will make you interesting as well. This will make it easy for you to attract the attention of other people, sell your ideas to them and even easily convince them to buy into your ideas.

Develop new skills

Having a set of skills especially those that people might not ordinarily associate you with can go a long way in making you more interesting. For instance, you might be the manager of a company but one day, you reveal your high-level culinary skills during a team-building retreat. Your colleagues at work will really find this interesting and they might even be willing to invest their time and money in developing similar skills.

Furthermore, having a set of skills that are relevant makes you a reliable person who others to those around you. Skills such as plumbing, web design and even culinary skills will make you the go-to-guy with respect to your colleges, neighbors and family members. Once people are willing to rely on you for solutions and pay you for your time, you will be on your way to becoming a successful human being.

Be open-minded

One way of driving other people away from you is by being a closed-minded kind of person. When you are not open to hearing the opinion of other people and their perspectives on things, then they are most likely to avoid your company since they will not find you interesting enough. On the contrary, when you are an open-minded individual, who is genuinely interested what others have to say, other people will find you interesting and will be willing to be around you and also listen to what you have to say.

Be curious about others

In order to be an interesting person, you must not be self-absorbed. People will find you more attractive if you are curious about their lives. To this end, you should always ask people personal questions that will allow them to tell you more about who they are for example, where they live, their hobbies and their views on certain issues such as religion. If you are able to do this, then you will be a much more interesting person by making people around you feel noticed and appreciated.

Try not to appear to be a know it all

No one likes a person who appears to know everything. People usually prefer the company of someone who is able keen to learn something or two from them. Even if you are the most learned person with several PHDs, the fact of the matter is that you cannot know everything. Even when you are interacting with people who are seemingly not at your status in life, you should always go out of your way to learn something or two from them. So as much as it is important to talk and share your stories, it is equally important to shut up and listen to others as they tell you something that you probably might not know.

Develop a sense of humor

Ultimately, it is almost impossible to be considered an interesting person if you have close to zero sense of humor. People will find you interesting if you are able to appreciate the lighter side of life from time to time. For instance, in case someone cracks a joke and you find it funny; do not hesitate to laugh out loud. But you should also be genuine in your quest to establish a sense of humor, there is nothing more annoying than a fake laugh.

Spend time with people who are interesting

It is very easy to become interesting by spending time with people who are also equally interested. This is because, even if you are not that interesting, the attribute might rub off on you and you might end up becoming a more interesting person in no time. For instance, hang around people who have an optimistic outlook in life, people who are open-minded and people who have a high sense of humor.

All in all, one of the simplest approaches to becoming successful is by making you an interesting person. When people find you interesting, they will be willing to associate with you and even go a step further and invest in you. Several things you can do in order to make you an interesting person including making other people feel like they know you, sharing interesting stories, develop new skills, be open-minded, be curious about other people and even spend more time in the company of other interesting people. If you are able to implement all these suggestions in your day to day life, then you will have commenced your journey to becoming a much more interesting person and this will significantly enhance your chances of success in life.

It is also equally important to remember that success does not necessarily mean financial success, but you can also attain success in other areas by applying some of the aforementioned strategies. For instance, you can improve your relationships with your friends, family members and significant other and all these are good examples of success in life.

Chapter 8: The Power of Metaphor

Language is one of the most reliable tools for communicating. Language is particularly vital when it comes to literal communication whereby what is said is what is actually meant. However, there are additional features of language that seek to make it more interesting with one such feature being metaphors. A metaphor is essentially a figure of speech in which the words are used to infer indirect connotations with something else. The metaphor thus renders deeper meaning to language and serves to make it quite beautiful.

One of the reasons why metaphors are highly preferred is that they create empathy and harmony. For instance, standing in someone else's shoes is a metaphor that seeks to create harmony in society. The literal meaning is to try to relate to someone else's situation. When it comes to metaphors and language use, there are those that are regarded to be quite common in terms of usage. Similarly, there are other metaphors that are also not very popular and it is generally best to avoid them. This article will analyze the role of metaphors in everyday language use and as well as highlighting the most commonly used metaphors and those, that should be avoided.

Metaphors in communication and empathy creation

Clear communication is vital when it comes to your capacity to empathize and understand the situation that another person is going through. Metaphors make it possible to use linguistic tools to enhance the overall clarity of communication. By using these tools, one is able to clearly demonstrate some of the challenges that a person can be going through because of their status or position in society. For instance, 'a black sheep' is a metaphor that can be sued to denote a person who is alone in terms of their difference from the rest. The metaphor is quite strong and can be used to elicit empathy since one can relate to this scenario in which you are in a group of people but you are singled out for being different.

Foster understanding

Metaphors can also be used to foster understanding and harmony. There might be various situations that at first glance might seem confusing. However, a good metaphor might render deeper meaning to them thus enhancing understanding. For instance, someone might be faced with a seemingly harsh destiny, for instance, a death row inmate or life sentence convict. At first glance, it seems quite harsh when one is faced with the prospect of imminent death or having to spend the rest of their lives in a confined room. However, an appropriate metaphor such as one who lives by the sword must die by it. This very strong metaphor simply means choices have consequences that are related to them.

Metaphors in an expression of emotion

Metaphors can also be used in the expression of human emotion. Human emotion refers to strong feelings that are times difficult to capture using mere words. For instance, you can say someone is annoyed but this might leave one hanging. One might be left asking themselves questions such as how much annoyed was he? A simple word might, therefore, fail to fully capture the range or extent of the human emotion in question. For this reason, metaphors can also come in handy in explaining the extent of human emotion thus making one to clearly appreciate the nature of the situation. For instance, a good example would be to say someone is on cloud nine. In essence, this is not a practical expression since to put someone in a cloud and specify the number of the cloud is impossible. But nonetheless, this metaphor does a lot in terms of capturing and conveying exactly how the person must have felt. To be in cloud number nine refers to someone being extremely happy and therefore the level of happiness could be quite high this is why they are literally being compared to someone who is up there in the highest cloud possible.

Popular Metaphors and Their Usage

Inspirational metaphors

These are metaphors that seek to inspire others. Inspirational metaphors make one yearn for more in terms of pursuing opportunities and overcoming challenges in life. A person is considered an inspiration to others if they are able to do something that is extra-ordinary. This is because; people will only look up to other people who have been able to rise above their expectations of society.

He is a shining star

This metaphor refers to someone who has performed exceedingly well in a certain area. A star is considered one of the most attractive heavenly bodies that are capable of standing out from the rest. This is considered a very popular metaphor in everyday language use. It is an expression that denotes excellence and it is also used to encourage people to work extra hard in whatever it is that they do in life. A person who is described as a shining star is therefore considered someone to be admired by others and looked up to as a good example to the rest.

The world is a stage and all people are nothing but players

Sometimes, metaphors can be used to enhance understanding of a phenomenon. These are things that are ordinarily beyond human understanding but they can be explained away using these unique language tools. For instance, 'the world is stage and all people are merely players' is a metaphor by renowned writer William Shakespeare. The world or global society as we know it today is perhaps one of the most complex eco-systems to ever exist. No amount of words can effectively define the world, which comprises of millions of living organisms, physical features, and synthetic artifacts. To this end, the author used a simple but effective metaphor to describe the world as a stage which is a description that adequately covers the world and everything that is in it. In this context, the metaphor uses a very simple definition to describe a very complex subject and thus makes it easy for just about anyone to understand what it is being described.

To be a high flyer

A high flyer is a metaphor that describes a high potential individual. This is someone who is likely to enjoy an elevated status in society on account of their academic or corporate achievements. For this reason, a high flyer is usually seen as someone who can go beyond the skies and realize goals and objectives that might be out of reach for an otherwise normal person in society.

Empathy – To be in another person's shoe

Various metaphors can also be used to relate to the manner in which another person might be feeling. As earlier stated, metaphors can also be used to elicit the feelings of empathy and compassion towards others. It is important for anyone to have a good understanding of some of the issues that affect other people in order to arrive at a common ground. To be in another person's shoes is a metaphor that enhances empathy and seeks to encourage people to have an open mind and see things from the perspective of others.

Lifestyle metaphors

People are unique and this uniqueness extends to the lifestyles they choose to lead. Lifestyle metaphors appreciate present the uniqueness of other people while at the same time highlighting some of the challenges that they might be facing.

You are nothing but a hound dog, crying all the time

Some of the most popular metaphors owe their status to the popularity of the people who first came up with these figures of speech. Popular culture is a term that refers to a system of organizing society around icons that act as trendsetters. Popular culture also lends itself to metaphors whereby some of the metaphors in use today are considered part and parcel of popular culture. One such metaphor is 'nothing the hound dog, crying all the time'. This metaphor is actually a title to a song by Elvis Presley, considered one of the most successful musicians of all time. The metaphor is used to describe a person who comes out as needy and a handful to deal with. Such a person, therefore, needs a lot of attention and this might a toll on anyone associated with them.

He is a couch potato

A couch potato is also another metaphor that has a negative connotation. Generally, this metaphor refers to a person who is regarded as lazy. A couch is a comfortable seta that is used for resting. Being a couch potato is thus someone who spends a lot of time sitting down and not doing anything particularly useful. Laziness is considered a negative attribute and when you refer to someone as a couch potato, then might take it as an insult. However, such a metaphor can only be used in you want to evoke a strong reaction on the part of the individual in question and encourage them to appropriate adjustments to their lifestyles.

Chaos is a friend of mine

People lead different lifestyles according to their situation. There are people who might lead peaceful lives while others lead lives that are considered more conventional. 'Chaos is a friend of mine' is a metaphor that was first used by English Rock Star artist Bob Dylan. Like a Rock Star, he leads a lifestyle that entailed many activities and this metaphor sought to highlight this lifestyle. 'Chaos is a Friend of Mine' is a metaphor that makes reference to a person leading such a lifestyle those others might see as confusing and not in line with the lives of ordinary folks.

Love metaphors

Love is considered a special kind of emotion that can evoke strong emotions on the part of many people. Some of these emotions might be positive emotions such as happiness, joy, and contentment. On the other hand, love can also result in negative emotions on the part of the lovebirds with some of the negative emotions being sorrow, sadness, and heartbreak. For these reasons, there are thousands and thousands of metaphors that are specifically meant to address the issue of love and how it affects the lives of many people. Love metaphors serve to bring out the different perspectives associated with this emotion.

When it comes to love metaphors, most of these metaphors relate to the romantic kind of love. Romantic love is considered a key area of interest because it is the kind of love that elicits the strongest response and emotions on the parties involved. Furthermore, romantic love is considered a mixed bag in terms of experiences. This is because they are many people who have had an experience that is deemed positive with respect to romantic love. Equally, there are as many people who have experienced negative emotions occasioned by this kind of love.

Love is fire

'Love is a fire' is a good example of a love metaphor that clearly seeks to adequately describe the emotion that is associated with being in love. A person who is deeply in love is likely to experience intense feelings and emotions and it is this intensity that has seen love being compared with fire.

Love is journey

'Love is a journey' is also another love metaphor whose usage seeks to enhance an understanding of the overall experience associated with love. A journey is an event that takes a considerable amount of time to accomplish. Furthermore, a journey might involve different stages from the start to the end. In comparison, true love is seen as something that does not develop in a spontaneous fashion; instead, it involves different stages at different points in the lives of those involved. Being in love also entails going through a myriad of experiences and it is such experiences that make up the entire journey that is love.

Love is a garden

'Love is a garden' is another love metaphor that seeks to capture the essence of strong emotion. In a practical sense, issues to do with love are complicated and must be accorded the attention that they deserve. This is the reason why love is compared to a garden. A garden must be tended to in order for the flowers in it to flourish. Equally, a relationship between two people in love should entail; both parties taking their time and attending to the needs of the other person in order for their relationship to succeed. This is indeed the reason why love is compared to a garden since, in order for it to flourish, it must be attended to.

Love is a flower

Love is a flower is deemed to be a pessimistic outlook with respect to the strong emotion that is love. This is because a flower is most often than not considering a very delicate plant that flourishes and becomes beautiful over a short period but then dies off soon afterward. Equally, they are those people who think that love and romantic love for that matter, is an emotion that is strongly experienced during the initial stages of a relationship but fades soon afterward.

Love is a battlefield

The final love metaphor of love is 'love is a battlefield'. 'Love is a battlefield' is an equally pessimistic metaphor when it comes to its perspective on the strong emotion that is love. In this context, love is being compared to a place, scenario or situation that is inherently uncomfortable. A battlefield is a place in which people are fighting or engaging in one form of conflict or the other. The metaphor, therefore, sees love as something that can bring many conflicts in the lives of those involved. The role of the parties to the relationship is to constantly address such conflicts hence the comparison to a battlefield.

Unpopular metaphors

There are metaphors that are considered unpopular with respect to their usage. The reason why such metaphors are unpopular is that they might offend someone of a specific category of people. For instance, some of these linguistic tools might have racist connotations while others are designed to offend the specific individual that they refer to. The usage of unpopular metaphors might be very controversial and for this reason, they are not generally preferred.

Black or grey metaphors versus white or light metaphors

One of the most controversial topics today is racism. Racism refers to the practice of undermining other people based on their racial heritage. Most often, their light-skinned counterparts have discriminated against dark skin people. For instance, African Americans were brought into the United States as slaves to work in white-owned farms and estates. Furthermore, colored skinned people such as Mexicans continue to be discriminated against in predominantly white societies and this is a good example of present-day racism. A racist mindset is one of the advocates that their own race is somehow superior as compared to the races of other people.

The issue of racism is also quite evident when it comes to metaphors and their usage. This is particularly the case when it comes to people's black metaphors versus white ones. In general, black metaphors are used to depict something that is bad and negative in society. On the contrary, while metaphors are meant to depict something that is good or accepted in society.

The black sheep of the family

The black sheep of the family is another metaphor with negative connotations. Ideally, this metaphor refers to someone or who is uniquely different from the rest. In the real-life scenario, being different can relate to both the positive and negative sense. However, referring to someone as the 'black sheep of the family' is mainly meant to portray them in a negative sense. This, therefore, implies that a person who is referred to in such a manner is not really a good person in terms of their character. Similarly, such a person might have deficiencies that make them naturally unattractive to others hence the connotation 'black sheep'. The 'black sheep of the family' is, therefore, a metaphor that should not be regularly used unless in unique situations that call for such reference.

Black market

A 'black market' is also another metaphor that might have racist connotations. This metaphor refers to a marketplace that is unsanctioned. In many cases, the black-market is described as a market where illegal and contraband goods are traded. Sometimes, the 'black-market' is the market where people go for products such as hard drugs such as cocaine and heroin. The racist association can be underscored by the fact that 'blacks' is also a term that is generally used to refer to African American people.

Gray area

'Gray area' refers to an area that presents an element of confusion when it comes to ordinary usage. A gray area is not really meant to be a good thing since people like to have an understanding of the issue that they are addressing. As a color, gray is the darker shade that is quite close to black and some might perceive the metaphor gray area as a metaphor that uses color to depict an unwanted and unfavorable situation that one might find themselves in.

Light at the end of the tunnel

On the contrary white or bright metaphors most often than are used to depict something positive. One such metaphor is 'light at the end of the tunnel'. This metaphor represents some degree of hope when it comes to its normal everyday usage. When someone says that there is 'light at the end of the tunnel' implies that they expect that something positive is going to happen notwithstanding the difficult situation that they might be currently facing.

White elephant

A white elephant is also another color-related metaphor that might be interpreted as racist. However, this metaphor is quite different from the aforementioned examples since it uses the color white as opposed to black. This implies that 'white' people might also have some sensitivities when it comes to metaphor usage since a 'white elephant' depicts an undertaking that is negative and one that has no benefit to the society.

Dead metaphors

Dead metaphors also generally fall under the category of unpopular metaphors. Precisely, these are metaphors that might not have a semantic rendition within the context of the present-day world since their usage is considered outdated.

Raining cats and dogs

When it comes to metaphors, one can also make reference to a special category of metaphors referred to as dead metaphors. As the name suggests, this is a group of metaphors that are no longer effective in terms of their capacity to relate to a context that they were originally meant to relate to. The existence of dead metaphors implies that as a figure of speech, metaphors relate to everyday life and experiences. They can only be effective if they are relatable within the context of the people using them. Some of the examples that are considered dead metaphors include 'raining cats and dogs' and 'a heart of gold'. Furthermore, when metaphors have not been in use for so long, they might end up falling under the category of dead metaphors.

To kick the bucket

To kick the bucket is another dead metaphor that literally means to die. When it comes to death, several other metaphors are generally preferred such as to 'pass on' to 'meet one's demise.' The reason why such a metaphor is not preferred is that many people might not really understand the connection between kicking a bucket and death thus rendering the expression unpopular.

Conclusion

To sum it all up, metaphors can be described as figures of speech or linguistic tools that entail one object that is used to refer to another one or an activity. There are various reasons why metaphors are considered essential linguistic tools. They serve to create empathy on the part of the listener. A metaphor can make you relate to the situation that is being described. These linguistic tools also play a key role in enhancing understanding of the issue that is being described. Metaphors also make it easy to capture human emotion since it might be very difficult to so suing ordinary words, but unique expressions such as 'being on cloud nine' can help you get the job done.

Several metaphors are used in various expressions and communication. Some of the metaphors can be described as popular metaphors since they are mostly preferred over others. Popular metaphors are easily relatable since they can easily be applied in contemporary life scenarios. Some of the popular metaphors include: To be a shining star, to be a high flyer, and to be in another person's shoe. Some popular metaphors have been used for hundreds of years but are still considered relevant in the present-day scenario. Furthermore, love metaphors such as 'love isa fire' are also quite popular. Similarly, there are also metaphors that are considered unpopular such as Black sheep of the family, black market and white elephant. Such metaphors can be deemed to have racist connotations hence their unpopularity. Finally, dead metaphors that have lost their semantic connotation also fall under the category of unpopular metaphors. A good example of a dead metaphor is the expression of raining cats and dogs.

Chapter 9: Learn To Manage Your Inner Dialogue

Your inner dialogue refers to that internal voice that seems that seeks to tell you what to do and when to do it. The inner dialogue affects how people think and their capacity to differentiate between right and wrong. One of the key differences between an ordinary dialogue and the inner dialogue is the fact that the former is open communication with other people, while the inner dialogue takes place internally either consciously or subconsciously. Furthermore, the inner dialogue is an endless undertaking where you are subconscious or inner vice keeps on talking to you in a more or less non-stop fashion.

There are people who pay a lot of attention to their inner voice while others do not pay as much attention. Nevertheless, it very is important to know how to go about managing your inner dialogue. Managing that voice inside you is very important especially when it comes to ensuring that you have the capacity to manipulate situations in your favor. Sometimes, going with your inner voice might be the logical thing to do but at other times, your inner voice might actually end up guiding you in the wrong direction. Managing that inner voice is, therefore, a delicate process that should be mastered and implemented in a cautious manner.

The main difference between human beings and animals is that human beings are guided by both their primal instinct as well as an inner rational voice. On the other hand, animals only rely on their primal instinct as the basis of their reaction to various situations. One of the reasons why it is important to manage your inner voice is, therefore, to differentiate yourself from other animals. This simply implies that you should learn to make rational decisions in each situation.

How Your Inner Dialogue Can Lead To Overall Happiness

Maintain positive thoughts

Management of your inner dialogue is vital when it comes to determining the quality of life you are able to lead. A good inner dialogue that encourages you to see the world in a positive light will translate to higher levels of satisfaction as well as happiness. In light of this fact, it is very important to ensure that you are able to maintain positive thoughts and try and stay away from thoughts and situations that might undermine your overall well-being. The saying you are what you think is indeed true when it comes to the management of inner dialogue since negative thoughts attract negative outcomes in real life. For instance, if you spend too much time worrying about your financial situation, you might end up in worse state financially. This is because you will spend more of your time thinking about how broke you are as opposed to waking up and actually doing something about it. In the end, you will end up pilling up more debt and making less money, which will make you unhappy. On the contrary, you can opt to think about how your life is going to be like when you eventually improve your financial situation. This line of thought will compel your inner voice to come up with instructions and guidelines on what you can do in order to improve your situation. In turn, you will end up being much happier and contented with your life.

Focus on the present

Most often than not, your inner voice will tend to focus more on your past or future at the expense of your present situation. For example, a person who was doing very well in the past in terms of their social and economic lives will prefer to ponder about their former glory. Similarly, people will tend to avoid thinking about the present in case they are currently experiencing difficult times and unfavorable situations. Such people would rather spend time focus their inner voice on what they think their future would be like. The harsh reality in life is that your past is gone and your present activities will determine your future. This implies that when you spend too much time thinking about the past, you will be wasting your time since there is nothing you can do about it. You will thus end up feeling unhappy and dissatisfied with your situation. In the same breath, when you spend too much time thinking about your future, you will not have time to focus on your present. This, therefore, implies that you will not be able to do all that you are required to do in order to maximize your current potential. When you fail to attain your full potential in the current sense, then your potential will equally be undermined.

On the contrary, if you spend much your time focusing your inner voice in your current situation, you will be in a better position to improve the same. If you are able to improve your current situation, then you can also safeguard your future. For instance, you might be able to come up with a viable business idea that will see you establish a very profitable venture that will improve your income both in the present and in your future life as well. Similarly, you might be spending too much time thinking about a failed relationship in your past instead of focusing on your present. If you instead spend more time in your present as opposed to your past, you will find a potential mate and you might end up being much happier than you used to be.

Focus on what you have

Your inner dialogue can serve to enhance you or destroy you. When you focus too much time asking yourself many questions about why your neighbor has something that you lack, then you might end up being unhappy. It is a fact of life that at any one given time, there will be people who will be better than you and others worse than you. This implies that if you want to spend your time thinking about what you do not have but others have, you will never experience a shortage of things to ponder about. However, when you look keenly at yourself, you will realize that you are abundantly blessed in both the material and non-material aspects. For instance, you might ask yourself questions and look down upon yourself because you do not drive a fancy car. But if you focus on what you have, you might realize that you have a lot more than that person you think is better off because of the make of their cars. Your friends, family members, and even career are things that you cannot put a price tag but you might often be tempted to overlook.

Focusing on what you have as opposed to what you think you should have, eliminates unnecessary worries and negative emotions such as envy and jealousy. It is also important to note that when you focus on what you have, you can identify ways in which you can apply the resources at your disposal to gain that which you do not have. Ultimately, focusing your inner voice on what you have is the best approach to maintaining a happy life and even achieving much more in life.

Learn to stop the negative internal dialogue

Sometimes, that inner voice might spiral out of control and go on overdrive in an attempt to convince you to make a decision that you know you will end up regretting. This happens occasionally when you come across a situation that is very tempting but one that will nonetheless translate to dire consequences. If this happens, then you owe it upon yourself to take the necessary corrective measures that will ensure that you do not end up regretting it in the future. In case you experience such a scenario, it is best to remind yourself to stop whatever it is that you are doing. In some cases, you might actually have to say this out loud for it to have the desired effect. By talking to yourself and reminding yourself to stop pursuing a dangerous course of action, you are likely to end up redeeming yourself from a situation that would have translated to great sorrow and sadness on your part.

Learn to forgive yourself

No one is perfect and this is certainly so when it comes to your capacity to always make the right decisions with respect to your inner dialogue. There will be times when your inner voice might lead you astray. In such a situation, one of the most important inner dialogue management measures is learning to forgive yourself. There is no sense in being too harsh on yourself on account of a mistake that you made attributed to that inner voice. You insist on beating yourself too much about it, you might end up feeling dejected, sad and lonely. It is important to constantly remind yourself that everyone makes mistakes but the most important thing is to learn from such mistakes. This implies that in case you realize that you have been misguided by that inner voice, the best thing to do is to accept the mistake, forgive yourself and promise yourself to do better next time around. By doing this, you will avert a situation where you end spending too much time regretting what you did and forgetting to think about what you can do in order prevent such an undesirable event occurring in future.

Be aware of the existence of that inner voice

It goes without saying that you cannot manage something that you are not aware of its existence. In order to effectively manage our inner dialogue, you must be aware that it does indeed exist. There are those people who might find it easy to dismiss such an existence and for such people, management of that inner voice will be an issue. They will invariably end up being controlled by the voice inside them.

You can learn the existence of your inner dialogue in several ways. One such method is engaging in a meditation exercise. Meditation is an activity that relaxes the brain making it easy for you to focus on your inner voice. Meditation also enhances overall concertation levels and such deep concentration can be effective in assisting you to make that much-needed connection with your inner dialogue.

A simple meditation exercise might entail simply sitting in a quiet room, switching off your phone and any other thing that might distract you and just allowing your brain to relax without focusing on anything in particular.

Be positive about others

Your inner dialogue is a very important tool when it comes to how you think about not only yourself but also other people. One of the ways through which your inner dialogue can improve your overall quality of life is when you go out of your way to maintain positive thoughts about other people. This is because the manner in which you think about others will have a huge impact on how you relate to them in real life. It is therefore important to keep reminding yourself that most people including your friends and family members are inherently good despite some of the disagreements you might have had with them. Try to focus on the good things that other people did for you and do not spend too much time thinking about the negative ones.

Sometimes, it might even be helpful if you keep reminding yourself telling yourself positive things especially when you are tempted to have negative thoughts about others. For instance, you can keep reminding yourself that 'he is a good man' in case a male friend or colleague of yours has disappointed you. Similarly, you can keep reminding yourself that 'she is a good kid' whenever you experience some sort of conflict or the other with your daughter. In both cases, your inner voice will ensure that you are able to maintain positive relationships with friends, family members, and significant others despite the myriad of issues that you might experience with them.

Do not spend too much time thinking about yourself

Many times, your inner dialogue will mainly focus on you as a person. However, you should avoid the temptation to spend endless hours just thinking about yourself. In fact, only self-centered people will spend a lot of time thinking about themselves but very little time thinking about others. Furthermore, it is often said that after all is said and done, people will remember you for what you did for them and not for yourself. Some of the bets celebrated individuals such as Mahatma Gandhi, Nelson Mandela and President Abraham Lincoln of the United States do not owe their status to what they did for themselves. They are considered exceptional human beings because of what they did for other people.

Your inner dialogue has the potential to make you an exceptional person or turn you into someone who is nothing but ordinary. You do not have to match the achievements of some of the aforementioned global icons, but in your own little way, you can be very exceptional to those around you. In order to this, you must encourage your inner voice to focus your attention on the welfare of others and not just yourself.

The question that you might be asking yourself right about now is, how do I go about to focus my inner voice on others? Well, a first step could be asking yourself several questions that touch on the welfare of the people around you. For instance, in case you notice one of your friends is increasingly becoming withdrawn, you can keep on asking yourself questions to this effect such as, 'why is Adrianna so sad these days or why does Ryan get easily offended nowadays. By doing this, you will encourage yourself to start thinking about the overall wellbeing of the people who matter in your life and even come up with solutions to some of the problems that they might be facing.

Extend your thinking to include the society

The society in which you live plays an important role in determining not only your welfare and the welfare of all the people in it. However, not many people spend a significant amount of time thinking about society. A better society will translate to better lives for all those in it and even for future generations that will have the privilege of living in such a society. On the other hand, a mismanaged society will translate to a myriad of problems for its current and future generations.

In addition to simply encouraging your inner voice to focus on those around you, you can also extend this to the society that you live in. There are many ills taking place in society and the only reason why they keep on persisting is that people do not spend time to think about them. For instance, you might notice that there is an increase in incidences in gender-based violence and exploitation. In such a case, you can focus your inner voice on this topic by asking yourself some of the reasons behind this trend and are the potential solutions. You might end up highlighting the issue and even come with noble initiatives such as the 'Me Too' movement that was probably occasioned by one person using their inner voice to focus not only on themselves but on the plight of others as well.

Image: words draws one to others or evoke rejection

One of the issues that are increasingly facing global society is global warming. Be that as it may, very few people even take time to focus their inner voices on such issues that are being experienced on a global scale. You and your inner voice can choose to be the starting point as far as addressing such global catastrophes is concerned. You can decide to spend some time each and every time thinking about the phenomenon that is global warming and what you can do in order to raise awareness and capture the attention of the powers that be. By doing this, you might even end up realizing the full potential that can come about when you effectively manage your inner voice and thoughts. Precisely, focusing on such grand issues affecting society can make you a global activist and might juts end being a truly exceptional human being recognized all over the world for your positive initiatives. This also illustrates that your internal dialogue is a powerful tool that can change the world.

Have a resolute opinion on issues

As a human being, you have the freedom to think about whatever it is that interests you. However, this freedom does not mean that are expected to accept the pre-determined positions of other people on issues that affect society. Many issues affect the world today including some of the aforementioned ones such as global warming, gender-based violence, racism, and hatred. These are very issues that have managed to elicit a lot of debates on many quarters as people talk sides and try to argue their cases. These debates should also be extended to your inner dialogue. Your inner voice should be able to raise such issues, debate on them and eventually enable you to have a resulted opinion that is informed by your own personal values and beliefs.

Many people end up confusing themselves because they have failed to formulate an opinion on an issue that is affecting them. For instance, the issue of racism continues to be a thorny one in many western nations. Effective management of your inner dialogue will allow for personal conservation on the issue, its underlying assumptions and even its historical underpinnings. By doing this, you will be able to come up with an informed and resolute opinion. However, if you fail to effectively engage your inner dialogue, you might end up being easily swayed by the prevailing assertions that might not necessarily represent the true position as far as these issues are concerned.

Take your time to learn how to master your internal dialogue

When it comes to mastering your inner dialogue, it is perhaps easier said than done. In reality, it is not very easy to regularly practice some of the aforementioned elements of mastering inner dialogue. For instance, it is not easy to totally avoid thinking about that fancy house or TV that your neighbor just bought. You might try and avoid thinking about it in your conscious mind, but your subconscious will always revert to this line of thought. Similarly, it is very easy to forget and even overlook that which you already have and instead, spend a lot of time thinking about what others have.

Ultimately, the art of mastering your inner dialogue is something that takes time and deliberate effort on your part. During the initial stages of trying to attain this feat, you are most likely to fail and end up resorting to your old habits. However, when you keep trying, repeatedly, your failures notwithstanding, then you will end up mastering the art of managing your inner dialogue. Furthermore, it is always advisable to constantly remind yourself of the need and importance of mastering your inner voice and thoughts. Once you are able to appreciate the fact that you will end up being much happier and satisfied with your life once you attain this feat, then you will find it much easier to go out of your way and implement some of the measures that will make you have greater control of your inner voice.

Conclusion

In summary, it is important to pay great attention to that inner voice that is inside that is otherwise referred to as your inner dialogue. You should always engage in inner dialogues that are well managed and ones that will serve to make you a better person. There are several ways you can go about managing your inner dialogue. First and foremost, you should strive to be a positive thinker and always see the glass as half full as opposed to it being half empty. Try to shun away from negativity and be aware of that inner voice especially when it is leading you towards negative thoughts and ideas. Secondly, try to think about what you have while pursuing your other goals and objectives. It is very easy to allow your inner voice to focus too much on what you do not have but this is not a productive undertaking. Managing of your inner dialogue also entails not being too harsh on yourself since everyone makes mistakes. In order to be a better person in both your immediate society and the global one as we, you think about other people as well as yourself. You must also use your inner dialogue to explore issues that affect global society and even come up with some of the potential solutions to address them.

Overall, effective management of your inner dialogue will make an attractive person to be with, enhance the quality of relationships you have with other people as well as making you an exceptional global citizen who will be admired by other people.

Chapter 10: Love Relationship

The Right Words to Use to Impress and Seduce Your Partner

Gone are the days when ladies fall for men with good looks or rather physical appearance. Nowadays, for a man to have the full attention of any lady, he must have a gift of sweet romantic words to convince her. Women love the world of fantasy and imagination, and that's why they prefer men who can drive them crazier with romantic words.

Sometimes, talking to attractive women is hard. Most men are not trained the art of talking to women and so, on the trial process, the following things might happen: they might make their women feel bored, they might be unable to attract the women of their dream, they might not keep their women interested in the conversation for a long time, they might fail to remain true to themselves around their women. Therefore, if you are unable to seduce women of your dream, then don't put blame on lack of popularity, money, power or looks. You must understand that women are not the same and so the styles of seducing women differ from one woman to another.

Seducing a woman with words of mouth is not a walk in the park, and so the following tips and tricks can better your seducing power.

Use soft and low tone

As a man, while talking to women with the aim of seducing her, your voice should remain soft and low. Loud and high voice scares off the women and generates fear on her. The moment a woman generates fear in you it shows your attempt failed because the woman will shy off from you. Therefore, while seducing a woman, it is advisable to use soft and low voice for it creates a conducive environment for you two and moreover, she might be flattered by your advance.

Lean as close to her as possible while talking

Leaning close to your woman is the most essential act while talking to her. It brings you two close and make her feel the words you vibe to her. Moreover, leaning close to your woman makes her feel cherished and loved and makes her feel that the seductive words are meant for her. In reality, this tip works better for many men. Therefore, men should put more emphasis on this and be more polite and gentle to the lady to be more attractive.

Try as much as possible to be witty and make her laugh always

A seducing man should not be offensive and try as much as possible to be humorous while talking to the lady. In your conversation, utilize more humor to always put a smile on her face. Most women love being taken out of their real-world to the world of fantasy. They say, this 'make their day'. Therefore, men should have a good sense of humor to make the women of their dream smile and be happy. This will make them absolutely irresistible to their men.

Always compliment her with simple yet effective words

For a matter of fact, jargon and overtly fancy words make women dull and angry always. Whenever they are angry, they feel offended so fast. To avoid this scenario, you should complement your girl with simple yet effective words to make her feel your presence always. Tell good things about her appreciate her always and speak positive things whenever you are together. For instant, if you like her curve then let her know openly; if you think her thought process is impressive then compliment her and let her feel that love you have for her.

Avoid focusing on her physical appearance while talking to her

It's truly hard not to focus and talk about her attractive physical appearance while talking to her. For men, their outlook and figure is always on their visual, but this is not the best thing to talk about when you are with her, trying to seduce her using words. The wise move to make at this moment is to avoid focusing on her physical appearance. Use romantic words relating to her positive character and personality. Therefore, while seducing your dream woman, most of your words should focus on praising her rather than mocking her. This makes her feel safe with you.

Confidence and composure can be really helpful

Most women nowadays go for confident men. Confidence and composure play a major role while seducing your girl for it makes a man stand out for himself. You have to keep your composure for the success of your seductive words. Over excitement spoils it all, and so it should be avoided and instead, confidence of the highest order should be maintained. Therefore, you should maintain calmness when you are with your woman. You cannot expect to impress a girl with just your words without confidence and calmness.

Smile and always maintain eye contact while talking

Actually, you must emboss this tip in your mind for it is the most significant point. A smile on the face creates an atmosphere for effective interruption. It makes your woman feel more absorbed by your actions. Maintaining continuous eye contact gives her the impression that you are really interested in her and that you need and care for her more than anyone else can do. Moreover, as you know, a smiling face is always appealing to anyone. Therefore, your physical appearance won't matter. So long as you try to put a smile on your face, that woman will one way or the other get attracted to you.

Try to appeal to her emotional side

Women have those emotional sides which make them sensitive and receptive. In this case, they have to be triggered and your conversation determines all. You have to make your conversation sweet and interesting in such a way that her emotional side gets triggered until it reaches the point where she starts feeling an attachment towards you.

Therefore, for you to seduce the woman of your dream suitably, you have to harness your conversation skills instead of freezing up in front of a beautiful and gorgeous woman. Make the environment around two of you flirtatious and fun so that you can eventually think of getting intimate with each other.

Chapter 11: Develop Humor and Make New Friends

Friendship happens as a result of connection at heart level. It is founded on trust. How do you start to build trust with someone you just met? Humor is one way. Laughter may be a means into the circle of trust. People who laugh less often earn less trust and it comes late. Laughter influences people to be more willing to disclose their personal information. When you share pleasure with people, a sense of intimacy is created and a bond is created between the two of you.

Humor creates an atmosphere of playfulness in which your counterpart gets primed to smile and join in the fun. When signs of stress and disagreement show up humor helps create a connection that provides a buffer against their effects. If you will make friends, you must first be friendly. The simplest way to demonstrate your friendliness is to tickle your senses of humor and make the people laugh with you. The more promptly you make people laugh the faster you make friends with them.

Meeting New People

Establish the conducive situations in which you are normally relaxed and at ease with yourself. Strive to strike friendships from there. You want to come across as naturally exuding humor and this can be achieved in your favorable environments. Attend local events that you are more involved with your community. You are more likely to meet people who share your interests in events that interest you. Besides, such events provide subjects upon which you can easily share views and interests.

Do join clubs that relate to your interests. The kinds of activities should be ones you enjoy. Strive to attend regularly to meet more like-minded people. Converse with them on what makes them join the club and see how promptly you get along. Volunteering to help with issues you care about also creates one such opportunity for you to connect with people who share your values. Are you song-trainer? Find somewhere to offer you skill for free with the view to connect with singers at heart.

Try out membership in recreational sports teams and in there occupy your space meaningfully. You cannot play in a team without interactions with your mates. In the spirit of teamwork, you will get to give and take from each other and create a mutual relationship that will build into friendships.

Fellowships in religious services or community initiatives also provide situations where you can meet new people of your kind.

Being in the right surroundings exalts your natural state of ease and authenticity. When you are there, do not hesitate to reach out for new associations. You do not have to begin out with a lot of effort. Just be sensitive to your environment and enjoy along. The others will follow or welcome you. Be willing to try new circles and see how much fun you can create or get beyond your comfort zones.

Fun Conversations

Introduce yourself to the people you meet as a conversation starter. Say your name and then something about yourself and ask them to their turn. Follow up with a comment on the situation at hand and allow them to react. Connect at the level of the event, and then dig deeper as the conversation advances.

Compliment them and keep them smiling for a while. People like it when you say good things about them. When you do so, they come across you as a nice person. Teach yourself how and always find a reason to give a compliment to your counterpart. Ask about the location or about the weather. It breaks the ice. This especially applies to people you just met. You need not make a lot of sense or say something important. Look around, pick on anything, make an observation and let them go on to comment about it.

Ask questions about them. Show interest in them. People love talking about themselves. Ask and easily get along with the conversation. What is more, listen in actively and you will be liked more. People want to be listened to. Ask open-ended questions and listen to their responses patiently ignoring any interruptions.

Make fun of yourself so they can laugh. On a light note, give a humorous reason why you arrived just on time and not slightly earlier or later. People do not like it when you take yourself too seriously. Go easy on yourself and they will be easy in return. Any of your quirks, mistakes, and things you like? Tease yourself on them and laugh along with others. Be mindful though not to ruin your demeanor.

Practice and learn telling jokes. There must be a few funny things or instances of your life. Do you remember any of your friends' or people's experiences that can create humor? Practice on them till you can deliver them naturally. Read and watch comedies and learn. Practice and mind the timing for the punchline in each joke. Be careful though not to disrespect yourself or others in the emotions of it.

Social Skills

What are your best qualities? Build your self-esteem on them. What are your distinguishing values? Evaluate your skills, talents, and interests and bring yourself out different from the rest. Appreciate your physical attributes too and play on them. As much as possible, invest in yourself and keep adding to your assets of personality. Build your confidence in these things and get into action meeting the world and what it gives.

Learn and always display an open body language. Smile, make eye-contact and tilt your chin up. Open body language tells others that you are approachable. It is inviting. Too, keep a good body posture and gesture along as you converse. Employ your conversation skills and look great at it. This may be learned over time. So do not judge yourself harshly if you are not there yet. Be a good listener as well. Avoid distractions and show your patience and discipline as a listener.

Go for what you want. Despite the laid procedures that we often observe to get certain things, you can purpose to find faster means there. Understand that it is not about procedures, but the results. Humor has a way of creating those shortcuts to peoples' hearts. Use it. Be yourself. You cannot come across great friends through acting, nor can you sustaining friendships in that way. Be honest with who you are and respectful to others.

Ultimately, humor is not about being funny. It is no comedy. It is about being lighthearted. Know yourself, dwell in the right places, meet the right people and do a little homework and you will soon realize how interesting space you occupy already is.

Chapter 12: Knowing How to Tell Stories

Tactics to Use to Capture Attention and Communicate Effectively

People have got brilliant ideas but they can't offer them to their prospective audience unless they have made it look come right first. You have to capture your target's attention before you can make her read or know how wonderful you are. Remember, your reader can't pay attention to everything. In order to understand the brain has to focus on specific information. Reader's mind is very selective, so you have to give them reason to pay attention to your content instead of everything else out there. Below are attention-grabbing strategies you should implement to fully curb your listener's or readers attention.

You must have a hook in your opening

In writing, this is called an inciting incident. To hook your listener with the story, you have to present a problem that encourages them to keep on listening to you. Once hooked, your audience may seek out more of your content getting to know you better. Creating a world in which it is taken away reveals the ultimate importance of this process. For instance, if you are explaining the concept of photosynthesis, try to bring out your story in a world in which all flowers didn't have leaves. This creates a problem that the story solves. You can always use this tactic in any lesson.

Every part of your story must be essential

When composing your storyline, for instance, fictional to teach a lesson or non-fictional, always try hard to connect each part of your story to the ending. Your character, points or principles must also relate the main point you are trying to bring out. Always listen to yourself and eliminate anything that affects your story be it directly or indirectly. For example, let us take the story about the planets. As a teacher you might be trying to help your students to memorize the order of the planets. Any tale you try to come up with to illuminate the facts must be related to the planets.

Draw a theme out of your story

It is very hard to write a story with a theme in mind, but a theme brings out the deep meaning of the story. It is rather advisable to first write the story elaborating all the points you want to cover. When you are done, stand back and see if you can draw out the theme of the story. Most probably this is important when your story relates to incidents in the past. Also apply real-life experience in your story because history can be boring. Themes always help to connect past with present and ultimately with the future.

Keep it simple

Complicated stories are always boring and aren't necessarily better. Consider your audience age bracket while telling your stories. When your audience comprises of youths, then just keep it simple. However, even older audiences can be profoundly impacted when you take a complex idea and reduce it to a nugget that can be remembered. Using complex vocabularies and scientific principles might be difficult for young minds. Try to bring out analogies because it can help for deeper understanding. For example, in explaining an electric circuit, describe how train can only move along tracks that are connected to each other.

Use vivid language that kids can understand

Human beings learn better through storytelling, and this has been proved by some psychologists. For instance, if you are teaching science or maths concepts, use a word or two that your students are unfamiliar with. Describe and define it then use it again and again. For example, talking of science, take the word energy and use it severally during your storytelling session. By the end of the lesson, your students would have understood the concept plus some other vocabulary. Most television channels and shows use this method. Using hard vocabularies unnecessary will reduce the power of your story. This is similar to reading texts in translation. When you want to have a deeper understanding of the content, you first learn the original language it was written in to carefully understand what the writer was trying to convey. So, if you want to use the right word, first explain it for your students to follow along.

Use dramatic pauses

Some people talk more quickly than their brain can process. Here pausing helps. Pausing at the crucial moments of the story helps the audience to think critically about the content you are delivering to them. A good storyteller should ease the pressure of tension by pausing. Most popular television shows use cliffhangers to bring the audience back into the story. At the moment you feel the problem is still unsolved, pause and give your audience time to think critically about the solution themselves. After each pause connect your storyline to the previous sentences and majestically kick-off.

Change your voice with different characters

Giving your characters different personalities make them more memorable. Part of this personality includes changing your voice when it comes to different characters. Beside visual props, changing of voice for different characters bring them o life. The best thing is to have different instructors to act as different characters. Sometimes it is difficult. For instance, let us take the case when you are re-enacting the civil war, stand tall and speak out as President Abraham Lincoln but when you are speaking as a Black American slave change your tone and use the accent.

Make the ending strong with an important takeaway point

The ending is the most crucial part and this is where most of the audience is up to. Put more effort into this part and whatever point or principle you feel is most important should be at this endpoint. If in case you already mentioned it at the content body part, and then just repeat it again to drive the point home. Most probably, make your ending sentence as short as possible. Use alliteration, repetitive words or even sing a song to make it more memorable. For example, if you want your audience to remember the theme of your story well, then come up with a phrase like "The civil war taught Americans that everyone is free to live, free to pursue their dreams and even free to be free."

Therefore, understand that stories are meant to bring meaning, feelings, and context to dry concepts. Invite your audience, give them enough to understand and follow along but not so much for spoon-feeding. Add drama, props, effects, and set the scene to draw your listeners into the story.

Chapter 13: Mindset

The Power of Positive Words

Positivity is something that is very essential when it comes to the day to day lives of human beings. Positivity basically means maintaining a positive mindset even in the face of adversity. Life will always bring forth a mixed bag of fortunes with some being positive while others can be described as negative or unfortunate eventualities. Nevertheless, it is very important to ensure that whatever situation you find yourself in, you are in a position to maintain a positive mindset through it all.

One way of ensuring that you are able to maintain a positive mindset is by appreciating the role and importance of positive words. Positive words are important when it comes to maintaining a proper relationship with both yourself and others. When you speak positively to others, there are more likely to like you and would go out of their way to seek your company. Similarly, when you use positive words when speaking to yourself, you are more likely to love yourself more and harness your inner strength in order to pursue your goals and objectives in life.

Repetitive use of positive words can improve the life of someone

It is often said that the tongue is a powerful tool that can serve to make or break. This simply means that the manner in which you speak to another person and the type of words you say to them, can either make or break them. When you repetitively use positive words such as telling someone they are good looking or they are important to you, then there will be more likely to feel very good about their own situations. Such feelings of enhanced self-importance will, in turn, propel them to reach out for more and confidently pursue their goals in life. On the contrary, sustained use to negative words towards another person can have the opposite effect of breaking them. I keep telling your friend or partner that they are not good enough or that they are not intelligent enough, you might end up breaking them. This is because; such negative words will result in feelings of inadequacy being ingrained in their psyche to the point that they will actually start believing your words.

Positive words can enhance your own self-esteem

Repetitive use of positive words is not only important when it comes to other people, but it also matters when you are having a conversation with yourself. It is very important to keep reminding yourself that you are important, you matter and that you are beautiful. Such positive sentiments will go a long way in enhancing your own self-esteem. This is particularly very important when you are experiencing difficult times since you are highly susceptible to negative thoughts at such times. Repetitive use of positive words in times of adversity will ensure that you are in a position to maintain a positive mindset even in situations that are difficult.

Many people are leading very sad lives because of low self-esteem. Such people are even afraid to pursue their careers and dreams in life because they think they are not fit enough to do it. For instance, a young woman might be very afraid to pursue their dream of being an actor because they think they are not beautiful enough. However, positive words especially when used repetitively while having a conversation with your inner self can change such a scenario. It is often said that self-vindication is perhaps the most effective form of vindication since it eliminates self-doubt thus making you a better person. Positive words can make you stop doubting yourself. You will stop looking for reasons why you should not do something and instead, focus on why you should do it.

For instance, you will remind yourself that you do not need to be the most beautiful person in the world in order to pursue your career as in the entertainment industry. All you need is the right amount of talent, determination, and zeal to pursue what you want. Positive words used repetitively will, therefore, enable you to improve your own self-esteem, go out, and pursue your dreams.

The role of positive words in enhancing your overall potential

Self-belief is a very powerful tool. Sometimes, you might sit back and wonder how people like Bill Gates and Warren Buffett managed to attain so much success in their lives. The answer is most often very simple, they believed in themselves. Such successful people had an idea and they believed in their own capacity to implement such ideas to the fullest extent. The role of self-belief when it comes to maximizing your success potential is, therefore, one that cannot be overstated.

Positive words also play a very important role when it comes to your own success potential. This is because; such words will improve your capacity to believe in yourself. For instance, if keep on telling yourself that you are the best at what you do, you might actually end up being number one. Some of the most successful athletes have also employed the use of positive words to propel them to unprecedented success. For instance, Jamaican born sprinter and global sensation Usain Bolt used to have the slogan 'Forever Faster' as the main source of his motivation. Such positive words of course along with other motivators ensured that he was able to obliterate world record and to this day, he is considered the fastest athlete in history. His achievements underscore the fact that the use of positive words even as personal slogans will, therefore, go a long way in guiding you towards attaining your dream.

Positivity rubs off on other people

The thing about positivity is that it generally attracts positivity. Simply put, a positive person is more likely to attract the company of other people who also happen to have a positive mindset. Furthermore, even if you attract people with a negative mindset, your own positive attitude occasioned by repeated use of positive words will rub off on them and make you have a better outlook in life. In light of this fact, it is important to ensure that you are able to repetitively use positive words both in your personal life and with others as well. Such sustained usage of words of encouragement and inspiration will ensure that you maintain yourself as a positive person and at the same time attract people with similar mindsets.

A pool of positively inclined individuals can be a very powerful force. When you are positive and are surrounded by positively inclined people, you are more likely to become with very good ideas on how to improve your personal lives. You will also benefit from enhanced synergy from people who would be more than willing to go out of their way to work hard towards the attainment of a common objective. Furthermore, you and the people around you will be in a better position to even go a step further to improve the society around you by making it a much better place filled with positive people.

Alternatively, one can argue that if you do not use positive words with yourself and with those around you, you are likely to end up attracting a pool of people with a negative mindset. A prevailing negative mindset will do a lot in terms of undermining your group dynamics and overall productivity.

Positive words can improve your physical and mental well-being

Everyday life can be too stressful. Getting up each and every morning, going to work, dealing with a rude boss and some of these everyday life issues might take a toll on many people. But the truth of the matter is, life is never and will never be a bed of roses. You will always be faced with situations in life that might seemingly be too difficult to handle. It can be very easy for one to decide to throw in the towel and decide that they will not take it anymore. In real life, this might see someone quit their job thus putting a significant dent in their careers. Others might decide to quit on a relationship that might have otherwise ended up being the best thing that ever happened to them. In some extreme cases, some people might even end up taking their own lives.

Positive words can go a long way in ensuring that you are able to come on top despite the day-to-day challenges associated with your life. You can wake up every morning and remind yourself that it is going to be a lovely day no matter what. In case you are faced in a difficult situation and one that you cannot immediately untangle from, such positive words like 'tomorrow will be a better day' will give you the strength and the zeal to go on hoping for a brighter future.

In all the aforementioned examples, the repetitive use of positive words will ensure that you do not fall into depression or lead an overly stressful life. This is because both depression and stress can result in other more serious health complications that can undermine your mental and physical well-being. By staying positive through repetitive use of positive words, you thus lead a much healthier life.

How to Use Positive Words in Your Day To Day Life

Complement those around you

Compliments are very powerful when it comes to improving the way other people feel. Compliments are basically positive words and expressions that are meant to point out something that is good about someone else. A compliment such as 'you have really improved in your performance this time around' is something that can encourage others to do even more. This is because the person will feel that whatever effort they have put in place has been recognized and appreciated.

When giving out compliments, it is important to remember to always issue genuine compliments. Genuine compliments highlight something that is actually positive regarding the other person. On the contrary, a compliment that is not genuinely such as telling someone that they have improved while this is not actually the case can pass for a lie. Once this person learns that you were lying to them, they might end up never believing what you say in the future as well as end up feeling bad about themselves. Secondly, you should always try and avoid the temptation to undermine the compliment by including a 'but' clause. For instance, telling someone 'you look good but not as good as the other guests'. Such compliments actually take away the intended positive message instead; it leaves the person feeling inadequate about their own lives.

Be aware of how you talk to yourself

It is very important to be wary of how you talk to yourself. The manner in which you talk to yourself will determine whether or not you are able to encourage yourself to reach out for more. As an individual, you should be able to appreciate the power of positive self-talk which is basically talking to yourself using positive words and phrases. For instance, whenever you realis that you have fallen below your personal expectations in a specific undertaking, you should tell yourself you can do better next time instead of saying 'that was very bad'.

Positive self-talk will ensure that you are in a position to dust yourself up and try again whenever you fail to meet your expectations. Moreover, positive self-talk can also go a long way in enabling you to convert your weaknesses into strengths. This is because you encourage yourself to no longer see perceive your weaknesses as impediments but as opportunities that can be explored for the benefit of both yourself and those around you. For instance, if some form of disability has afflicted you, you can use this as an opportunity to be champion for the rights of people affected with similar disabilities this benefiting yourself and others.

Come up with specific positive words that you will use

It might be virtually impossible to exhaust the vocabulary of positive words. There are many positive words that are out there but not all of them might be applicable to your specific situation. In light of this fact, you should be able to know those words that can work effectively with you and those that might not be applicable to your specific situation. By using positive words that specifically relate to your situation, you will find much easier to realize and appreciate the positive effects of such words.

Learn to think before you speak

One of the reasons why you might use harsh words on yourself and on other people as well is because you are in a hurry to respond. Sometimes, it is not always a good idea to always insist to respond to issues, questions, and queries in a hurry. Instead, you should exercise thinking before you speak. For instance, someone might ask you questions that might initially seem stupid. Your obvious and immediate reaction would be to respond in kind by issuing out a rather harsh response. However, if you are able to think before you speak, then you will be in a better position to find the right words to respond with. You will be more likely to use kind words and avoid a scenario where you offer an emotional response. A thoughtful response full of kind words such as 'may I suggest', 'may I refer you to' and other such words will ensure that your response attracts the attention of other people.

You could be wondering how long you should wait before offering your response. There is no rule of thumb when it comes to the duration of time that you should wait before responding to a question r query. Ultimately, the duration must be reasonable and one that allows for meaningful conversation. In essence, you can choose to wait for at least five seconds before responding. This is a typical duration that can allow you adequate time to come up with a good response and one that is full of positive words. However, the exact duration could be a little bit shorter or longer depending on the question and your understanding of the same.

One of the reasons why it is important to think before you speak is because people are different and unique. This uniqueness also extends to their individual sensitivities. Positive words and their usage play a very significant role when it comes to addressing some of the sensitivities that other people could be having. A word might seem simple in everyday usage but I might be considered very offensive to a specific category of people. For instance, the word midget can be very offensive when referring to little people. Positive words can enable you to select the proper word of vocabulary you can use instead of such offensive ones. Being able to think before you speak will enable you to identify the proper word to use in light of potential sensitivities that some of your audience members might have. IN this case, you might what to say little people instead.

Make regular use of kind words

Positive words go hand in hand with kind words. In fact, there are many kind words that are also regarded to be positive in nature. For this reason, you should always remember to use kind words in conjunction with positive ones. Words such a kindly, sorry, may I and please can go a long way in enhancing the overall quality of conversation that you may be having with someone else or even yourself. For instance, you can say 'that was very delicious, can I please have some more?' In this instance, you might congratulate the chef using positive words but the additional use of kind words makes the congratulatory message sound more sincere.

The use of kind words especially on a regular basis will also make you an attractive person. Kind words convey a feeling of warmth and approachability. For instance, whenever you use the word 'kindly' when requesting something, the other person is more likely to honor the request. This is because; your usage of such words will make them feel like they are dealing with a nice person who is approachable. Everybody wants to be around nice people even do things for them. To this end, people will always receive you much more positively and they will be willing to do things for you or with you hence making you an attractive person.

Learn to be thankful

Developing a habit of expressing gratitude for each and every good thing another person does to you is very important. When expressing gratitude to others, you will most often than not find yourself using positive words of encouragement. For instance, whenever someone offers your assistance with something small or big, you can say 'thank you so much, you were very helpful'. This is an expression of gratitude while at the same time, it employs the use of positive words such as you were very helpful to encourage and enhance the self-esteem of the other party.

You might often find yourself showing gratitude for the big things done t you but overlook the small ones. However, learning to express gratitude even for the seemingly small things will ensure that you develop a natural capacity to use kind words with others without even knowing it. This natural ability will make you an attractive person and at the same time. Furthermore, people feel much better about themselves whenever they are appreciated especially for small things. You will, therefore, be able to have a significant impact on the lives of many people without even knowing.

Many people might not know this but being thankful for the small things and favors you get is likely to open doors for bigger ones. For instance, you might ask someone for some small money in order to invest in a simple startup company. While returning the money, you end up expressing a lot of gratitude for the assistance they gave you. In case you ever need similar assistance in the future, they might be willing to give you even more. The enhanced generosity can be attributed to two things. First is because you obviously honored your promise to repay the money. Secondly and perhaps most important, is the fact that you were indeed very thankful when returning the money. On the other side, if you had just simply returned the money and offered a simple thank you, you might not enjoy the enhanced generosity next time. In this example, the power of positive words in expressing gratitude can improve your chances of success through access to more opportunities.

Learning how to use positive words

Repetitive use of positive words is undoubtedly a very important skill. However, in order to be good at it, you should take time this vital social skill. One of the steps that you can take in order to learn how to repetitively use positive words on others and on yourself is by listening to reading or listening to literature that is inspiring. There are many books out there and even audio files featuring an array of inspirational speakers. Such productions are always full of information about how you can go about marinating a positives lifestyle. Most of them emphasize the role of positive words and how repeated use of such words can result in an overall positive lifestyle. By reading or listening to such books, you will be in a better position to appreciate the role of such words and even learn many examples of positive words, which you can use in your everyday interaction.

Conclusion

Briefly, it is very important to stay positive at all times. Life can and will present you with challenges and difficulties that might be seemingly overwhelming. However, maintaining a positive mindset will ensure that you are able to overcome anything. Positive words go a long in enabling you to maintain a positive lifestyle.

Positive words are mainly wording of encouragement such as you are strong, you can do it or even you are beautiful. Such words are very powerful in enabling you to improve your self-esteem as a person. Improved self-esteem will make you stop doubting yourself and instead, you will be able to things that you thought you would never do. Positive words can also improve your capacity to attain your dream by reminding yourself that you are better than they are and that you have what it takes. You thus are able to attain your full potential.

Positivity is an attribute that easily rubs off on other people. By maintaining a positive lifestyle through repeated use of positive words, you will be able to make those around you to be positive about life as well. You will also be able to attract other people with a positive mindset. When you have a pool of positively minded individuals, your overall group dynamics will be enhanced thus improved productivity.

Your physical and mental well-being can also be improved through sustained use of positive words. Such words will ensure that you are not overwhelmed by whatever situation you might be facing. This will avert potential health complications occasioned by depression and stress. Finally, there are several ways through which you use to ensure that you are able to integrate positive words in your day-to-day life. They include complimenting other people, thinking before you speak, coming up with a list of specific positive words to guide you in your day-to-day activities, being thankful for others and being aware of how you talk to yourself.

Manufactured by Amazon.ca
Bolton, ON